Love, Hugs, And Kisses

A Daughter's Grief Journey

Karen L. Crouch

Saltbox Press
Spring Arbor, Michigan

Copyright 2002 by Karen L. Crouch

All rights reserved. No part of this publication may be reproduced, stored in a retrieval system, or transmitted in any form or by any means--electronic, mechanical, photocopy, recording, or any other-- except for brief quotations in printed reviews, without prior permission.

> Distributed by:
> Karen L. Crouch
> 1013 Duncan Avenue
> Cheboygan, MI 49721
> Email: ldcrouch@triton.net
> 231-627-4216

1 3 5 7 9 10 8 6 4 2

Published by Saltbox Press
167 Burr Oak Drive, Spring Arbor, MI 49283
Printed in the United States of America
Autobiography, Grief, Hospice

ISBN: 1-878559-07-9
Price: $15.00 USA

Love, Hugs, And Kisses

A Daughter's Grief Journey

Contents

Page	Chapter	
7		Introduction
9	1.	The Beginning
35	2.	Disconnected
49	3.	I Finally Unpack
65	4.	Getting Over This "Gone" Thing
79	5.	The Wringing Of The Cloth
95	6.	This Is Grief
103	7.	Gifts That Come
117	8.	The New Beginning
119	9.	Columns For Mom
129		Acknowledgements
131		Resources

Introduction

I was truly blessed as a daughter. In spite of a less than perfect marriage, her husband's alcoholism, and constant financial struggles, my mother managed to convey to her only daughter a sense of unconditional love. No matter what happened in my life, she loved me. Mom was my most ardent cheerleader in whatever I attempted. I know now, through my friendships with other women, that this was a rare and precious gift. Mom also shared with me her faith in Jesus Christ. During my adulthood, I watched her go from a woman who tended to keep such things private, to a woman who openly rejoiced in the strength she received from her Lord.

In the time since my mother's death, I have grown and matured. I am a stronger, better person, one I wish she had the opportunity to know. I have turned my lifelong scribbling and journaling into a weekly column with our local paper, and if Mom were here, she would say, "Isn't that wonderful!"

This book isn't just a tribute to my mother, but rather a tribute to the grief process that ensues from the loss of such unconditional love. It is my chronicle of the time preceeding her death, and the days and weeks following, when I was torn by grief. During that time, I could only find a few people who had experienced what I was going through. Because I was a grown woman, the death of a parent was considered a "normal" loss, certainly not the stuff of high tragedy.   There were times when I wondered if I was "abnormal" for grieving so hard. More than anything else I wanted to know that I wasn't the only one on the planet who had ever felt that way. I decided to keep a journal, knowing that the process of writing would help me in my pain. I also had a glimmer of an idea that someday I could share my process and perhaps ease the pain of someone else. This journal is for people at the beginning of their grief journeys who would appreciate knowing that they are not alone. It is also for anyone who is wondering if grief ever gets better. To these people, and of course to my mother, I dedicate this book.

1. The Beginning

Saturday, April 22

It is Saturday afternoon and the phone rings. I am not anticipating bad news. It is a telephone call from one of my mother's friends, Annie. Exactly eleven months after her first terrifying bout with congestive heart failure when she almost died, my mother has had a recurrence. This episode doesn't seem nearly as serious. She is in the hospital, but on a regular floor. It is daytime. Last time she was in the intensive care unit, on a ventilator, in the middle of the night. I was notified by a police officer pounding on our door, because for some reason neither my husband nor I heard the downstairs phone ringing. Annie tells me that this time Mom is stable, that the doctors just want her in the hospital to adjust her medications. I am able to telephone and speak directly to my mother, another change from last time. She sounds good, reassuring me that this is just "mild heart failure" and that she actually feels pretty good. Mom tells me not to rush down to Jackson now (four-and-a-half hours away), as we are already planning a trip later in the week to finalize our second son's adoption. I don't anticipate any problems with this, but just to be safe, I call my mother-in-law, Ruth. Larry's parents also live in Jackson County on a family farm. Ruth has helped me before, and I know I can count on her. More importantly, she is a retired nurse and I trust her opinion. I ask her if she would go to the hospital and eyeball my mother for me, and let me know if she thinks I should come down sooner. She reassures me that she will do this, and then call me with a report. Larry and I decide to keep life normal and participate in our weekly bowling league. During bowling I begin to feel uneasy, but I reassure myself that it is just normal concern. When we get home at 9:30 I call Ruth but don't get an answer. I consider calling the hospital, but before I can, the phone rings. It is Ruth, and I can tell by the sound of her voice that something's up. She tells me that things went from "serious to bad to worse." She was sitting by Mom's bedside around 8:00 p.m. talking with her. Suddenly my mom got nauseous and began vomiting. Before Ruth's eyes she became short of breath and turned blue. She was rushed back to intensive care, and is now, once again, on a respirator. Ruth, who is never an alarmist, sounds shaken and I am scared. I call my brother Russ, Mom's sister Aunt Ruby, and Mom's sister-in-law, Aunt Charlene. We all wait. I call the hospital frequently, and am reassured that for the moment, Mom is stable. By now I decide not to drive down to Jackson this late at night, and I make plans to go in the morning. I talk to my pastor, and to my group of friends and prayer warriors. They all comfort me by promising to pray, and I may actually get a little bit of sleep. *Dear Lord, please don't let Mom go into a vegetative state. I don't want to have to make those hard decisions.*

Sunday, April 23

It is a dreary day, and I leave Cheboygan by 7:30 in the morning. After much debate, I decide to go alone. Larry will stay with our boys since they are going to have a long trip later this week regardless of what happens with Mom. The boys are only five years and one year, and traveling is hard on them. We must go downstate to finalize Sam's adoption, and after more than a year of waiting there is no way we are going to postpone that. Mom would have a conniption if we did! My drive is uneventful and at the hospital I am relieved to see that Mom is stable. They plan to take her off the respirator soon. Aunt Ruby has made the trip as well, and stays by Mom's bedside for the day. Ruth wants me to stay at their house for the night, but I opt for staying alone in Mom's apartment. It is the only way I know to feel close to her. I also find her lockbox and begin digging through important papers. I sleep fairly well, tired out from worry and the long drive. I miss my guys at home!

Monday, April 24
    I wake up early, a miracle for me, a confirmed night owl! I arrive at the hospital in time to talk to Mom's doctor. Mom is stable, and off the respirator. She doesn't remember Aunt Ruby coming, and she doesn't remember much of the last 48 hours. I am reassured enough about her condition to head back to Cheboygan until Thursday. Aunt Ruby will stay with Mom until then. *Dear Lord, please keep Mom safe until I can get back to her, and help me stay awake for the long drive home!*

Wednesday, April 26
    Mom is still in the hospital. They wanted to do a stress test but she is too weak to walk. Instead, they did the drug-induced stress test and found that there is more coronary artery blockage than before. I am uneasy about her condition.

Thursday, April 27

    Larry and I drive separate vehicles to Ithaca, with the kids, to complete Sam's adoption. Ruth, Dale, and my Aunt Charlene meet us at the courthouse. I miss my mother. She was there at Nathan's adoption. Everything goes smoothly and Sammy is finalized into our family. Hallelujah! We have balloons and cookies at the courthouse and take pictures, and then leave for the rest of the trip to Jackson. Larry goes to the farm with the boys and his parents, and I meet my Aunt Ruby at the hospital. I get there just in time for Mom's cardiac catheterization. She comes through it fine. It showed that the blockage is up from 50% to 75%, still survivable. She will come home tomorrow while the doctors decide whether or not surgery is an option. She is weak and in severe pain from the arthritis in her back and neck. I finally leave the hospital and return to my in-laws' farm to spend the night with Larry and the boys. Larry and I argue over nothing. We are stressed and worried and taking it out on each other. There just isn't a lot I can do about it. I am physically and emotionally drained. I cry all night. *Dear Lord, thank you that Sammy is officially ours. Thank you that you are my rock and my hiding place. Help me through this. Amen.*

Friday, April 28

    I wake up in tears. I feel totally alone. Nathan is scared about Grandma and finds his way into our bed. Hugs and cuddles reassure him and help his mom and dad as well. A few tickles later and we are all laughing and I can start my day. After leaving Larry and the boys at the farm, I bring Mom home from the hospital. We have to use a wheelchair. Aunt Ruby stays with us until evening. Then my cousins Barry and Kathy come and take her back to her home in South Haven. I'm really glad that she's had this time with

Love, Hugs, and Kisses

Mom. Larry and the boys visit just before Aunt Ruby leaves. Now everyone has left and I've tucked Mom in. I am sleeping on the living room sofa. It is comforting to be alone with Mom.

Saturday, April 29

I'm having a good day with Mom. We've had lots of time to talk, although I've tried to convince her just to rest. My friend Jenny and Larry and the boys get here about 4:00 p.m. Aunt Charlene and Aunt Pat and my cousins Tim and Tom and their girlfriends arrive a little later. We have cake and pop in the lounge of Mom's apartment building to celebrate Sam's adoption. It isn't quite the party we had for Nathan's adoption, but under the circumstances, it is the best I can do. Jenny videotapes it all. People take turns going upstairs to see Mom. Larry still seems withdrawn. He is just restless, being away from home and work. I feel torn, celebrating Sam and worrying about Mom. It is a hard combination of feelings, and I don't like it!

Sunday, April 30

Annie is here to stay with Mom so that I can go out to the farm for yet another party. It is a combination adoption-birthdays-baptism celebration. With this big of a family, eleven brothers and sisters, plus in-laws and kids, it works better to combine the various celebrations. I try to put my worry aside so that I can enjoy the day. The cloud over my head lingers, but I hope it isn't obvious to everyone else. Larry is more relaxed because he is going home today. The boys will stay with my mother-in-law and I am thankful. I can stay with my Mom for the next week and try to work things out. I return to Mom's apartment at five and thank Annie for staying with her. Larry comes by about seven to say goodbye before he heads back home. He is doing much better and seems happy. *Dear Lord, please grant my husband traveling mercies and keep us all safe until we are together again.*

Monday, May 1

This morning the nurse from the Health Department is here to check Mom. It is good to see Marliss again, as she was Mom's nurse during her first illness. Mom has gained two pounds, probably all fluid. We have an appointment today with Mom's cardiologist, Dr. P. I am hopeful that he will be able to do something surgically to help her. <u>Monday afternoon:</u> What a letdown. The doctor said Mom isn't a candidate for surgery at this point due to her overall condition and her low blood pressure. I think he is trying to warn me. I don't want to hear it. I drive through McDonald's to get us each a chicken salad, but I don't really feel like eating. While Mom is resting, I make a bunch of phone calls to family and friends. Everyone is concerned. Can they tell that I am scared?

Tuesday, May 2

The Lifeline people are here this morning. Mom will have a button to push to call for help once I leave. I will do everything I can to make her safe before I head for home. I notice some forgetfulness on her part today, possibly some short term memory loss. What is causing that? Mom's friend Millie will come to stay with Mom this afternoon so that I can get out to the farm to see the boys. I could really use some little boy hugs about now!

Wednesday, May 3

The new Meals on Wheels people come this afternoon. The chore provider people will start next week. I get out to see the boys for an hour. Mom does ok by herself. Dr. K. calls today to check on

Mom. She is still in so much pain from her arthritic back and none of the medications have helped. She can't take any of the anti-inflammatory drugs because of her ulcer, and the Vicodin isn't touching her pain. I keep thinking that if she could just get some decent rest, free from pain, she might regain some strength. Dr. K decides to start Mom on a low dose of MS Contin and MSIR, long and short acting morphine just like we use in Hospice. He said her pain isn't going to go away, and she isn't a candidate for surgery, so maybe this will help. I hope so. I am worried about her ability to take her pills correctly.

Thursday, May 4
    Mom's friend Bea is here. It gives me a chance to tend to business. I know I have to go home soon. Yet I feel I can't leave Mom until I know I've done everything I can. I go to Dr. K and the pharmacy to pick up the morphine for Mom. Then I swing by the hospital and grab an advance directive. I think it is time to get all of her decisions in writing. I also manage errands and groceries, and stop at the farm to see the boys. Time goes too fast, but I get it all done. I worry when I am away from her. When I went to set up the medication tray I realize that Mom hasn't been setting up her meds correctly. I put on my nursing hat and rewrite her med list and reorganize her med cup system. I fix her supper, a simple one of chicken breasts, rice, green beans and watermelon. I make her a tray and decorate it with a garnish of strawberries. Mom always taught me that presentation is half the battle in making food appealing, and I have fun adding these little special touches for her. *Dear God, please help Mom be able to manage ok on her own and to take her pills correctly. Help me know when it is all right to go home. My guys need me too!*

Friday, May 5

I'm making plans to go home. Mom is feeling some pain relief since she started the morphine. Her speech is slightly slurred, but that should fade. My friend Sherri visits this afternoon. She witnesses the signing of the advance directive. It is good to have that done. I take Mom to Dr. K today. It went ok, but was exhausting. Mom is tired because we stayed awake talking so late last night. We've had lots of good talks this week. We've watched her lily plant every day, it is still blooming and she is so proud of it. Mom's never really had a green thumb, so this is fun. I also clean and organize her bedroom today. She hates having me do all of this for her, but I get her paperwork and her bills straightened out. Out of the blue Mom asks, "What happens if that artery clogs 100%? Is it all over?" I try to be reassuring about the medications she is on and their effectiveness. But this morning I made a private trip to the funeral home and did pre-planning. I didn't put any money down, but I got prices locked into place if we send money within a couple of weeks. I'll talk to my brother about it and see what he wants to do. I think we may have a year left with Mom. After the funeral home I stop at my friend Laurel's for tea and sympathy. She's been a bright spot this week.

Saturday, May 6

Bea is here. Mom seems a little fuzzy but not too much. I think she'll be ok. She has help coming in almost every day. She took her pills right yesterday and this morning. At this moment she is pain free and she slept well for the first time in months. I hate saying goodbye, but I have to. Mom thanks me over and over again for everything. I finally tear myself away. Leaving the building, I am panicked. I may never see her again. I reassure myself that of course I'll see her again, I am just being paranoid. I want to run back upstairs and hug her again. I decide not to because I don't want to scare her. We had lots of hugs this last week. There will always have to be one last one. The next time I see her may be another crisis and I'll hug her bunches then. I finally get home to Cheboygan about five p.m. I am now a mother again instead of just a daughter. When I call Mom tonight she sounds good. She hasn't needed any short-acting morphine since 11 a.m. and she is feeling good pain relief. Now I have to get used to being home. There are mountains of laundry to do!

Sunday, May 7

We make it to worship and Sunday school at our new church. Then we go out to dinner and see a bunch of our friends from our old church. It is great being back. At home I get a call from my mother-in-law, Ruth. Back to reality. Mom is confused and has fallen. She got her meds mixed up after all. Her home health nurse called Ruth when she couldn't reach me. I call Mom and talk to her. She knows me and knows what happened, but her voice is groggy. I call her friend Camilla and she is going to go stay with Mom. I call her nurse. Mom won't be able to stay at home alone, and we can't afford to pay for someone to take care of her. I will make arrangements for people to stay with her until I can go back to Jackson on Wednesday and then we'll talk about adult foster care. Ruth is checking into places for me. There is a nice place by the farm and that would be convenient. Ruth would also be able to keep on eye on things for me if we moved Mom there. I hate to move Mom out of her bright little apartment. It is the first safe stable home she has had since Dad left her after thirty-two years of marriage. The trailer they had bought brand new was cheaply made, and a few years after Dad left it began to fall apart around her head. My brother and I did what we could to keep it functional, but it was basically throwing money away. It was never really a happy home for her anyway. Then Mom lived with a friend for a while, but that was awkward at best. Living with us for about six months was a temporary solution, and then we got her into her apartment in the senior building. She has loved it, made friends, made a home. I hate to rip her away from that. *Please, God, help me do the right thing.* I call my brother and fill him in. He can't believe that Mom is in this much trouble. He wants me to call him once I have more information. I call Mom again at 4 p.m. Camilla is there and will spend the night. Mom got mixed up again and has already taken her bedtime meds. I talk with her. I want to cry. She thanks me again for all I've done and repeats over and over again that she loves me. I call again at 8 p.m. and talk to Camilla. Mom has slept for two hours and talks to me briefly. We say our "I love yous" and hang up. I call my friend Jenny in tears. I cry and ramble on the phone. I say, "I can't believe I am losing my mom this soon."

Monday, May 8

     3-4 a.m. I can't sleep. Sam wakes up crying and I sit rocking him in his bedroom. Even after he's back asleep I keep on rocking. I am in agony. I pray. *Please God, help us through this. If Mom can be spared this burden of moving, please do so. If not, please just help us through.* My insides are being shredded. I am scared. I want to be with Mom right now. Instead, I keep on rocking Sam. The phone rings at 7 a.m. "Hi, Karen. It's Ruth. Is Larry still home?"

     I know. "She's gone, isn't she?" I ask.

     Ruth answers, "Yes," and then asks if Larry is with me. He is. I try to hang up but Ruth says, "Wait, there's more you need to

Love, Hugs, and Kisses **19**

know." I cry and cry. She tells me to call Mom's apartment and talk to the nurse and the police officer. I do. Apparently Mom fell in the bathroom around midnight and Camilla called the ambulance. They got Mom back into bed because she refused to go back to the hospital. I am sure she was frightened and didn't want to face another round on a ventilator. Mom hadn't hurt herself and seemed to be coherent, so the paramedics left. Camilla slept sitting up in the recliner outside Mom's bedroom and never heard another sound. Mom's nurse got there at 6 a.m. to check on her and found her. She must have just quietly stopped breathing. The nurse thought she had probably been gone a couple of hours.

I wonder if she died when I was awake, rocking Sam, praying for her? I give the police officer permission to release Mom's body to the funeral home. Dr. K has already been called by Mom's nurse and he'll sign the death certificate. Mom's nurse has been a Godsend and so has Dr. K. I call Aunt Ruby and Aunt Charlene. Then I call my brother Russ. Gwen answers, Russ has already left for work. She will call him there. Telling Nathan is awful. Larry helps me hold him as he sobs. Then he takes Nathan to preschool before he goes to work so that I can get ready to leave for Jackson. I just keep crying. I am haunted. I should have said goodbye one more time. I should have gone back up to her apartment before I left Jackson. Why didn't I? I want that extra last hug. Now I can never have it. Was that only two days ago?

I call our old church. Friends come. Nata brings a card and money from the Bible study group that I lead. She does dishes. Kathy comes and Ellen comes. *Thank You, Lord for good friends.* I pack and leave the house at 1 p.m. I stop at the Co-Op to say goodbye to Larry. He will finish what he has to at work and then head for Jackson tomorrow. One of the employees gives me a card with cash from all of Larry's workers. She cries and so do I. People crying for my grief is an amazing thing. I stop at the deli for a quick take out lunch. I see one more friend who cries with me. Tears are precious. I hate them. I cry in the car off and on while the boys are asleep. It seems like an unreal trip back down a road I just traveled. I sing songs once we hit Jackson to try and keep my act together.

    Now it is beginning to seem real. I drop the boys off at Ruth's, thank her and get a hug. Then I head to Mom's. Aunt Charlene meets me there in the lobby. More hugs and tears, and then we see Mom's friend Bea in the meeting room. We talk and then head up in the elevator. I don't want to enter Mom's apartment. Her bedroom door is open and the bedsheets are rumpled. There is a wet spot on her pillow. I wonder what caused that. There is a strong smell of vomit. Camilla had said she was sick when she fell, maybe that's what the wet spot is. Maybe she aspirated some vomit and that is why she died. I fall apart.

    Aunt Charlene hugs me and lets me cry. Aunt Charlene does laundry and we clean a little--try to get rid of the smell. Mom should still be here. She just was, two days ago. How can she not be here now? The whole apartment is filled with her, but she's not here. We choose clothes and jewelry and make more phone calls. My brother is still traveling from Tennessee. We go to the funeral home and then Aunt Charlene takes me to supper at the old steakhouse, a Pahl family tradition. Soup is comforting. Then I head back to Ruth's for the night.

A Poem for Mom

You were just there, two days ago.
I said goodbye and closed your door.
I knew I would see you next time.

You were just there, two days ago.
Today I opened your door, you weren't there.
Not in your bed or your chair.
Not at the refrigerator getting ice.
Not down getting your mail.
I checked. I checked again.

You were just there, two days ago.
Pieces of you remain.
Your glasses, your pillow print,
Even your teeth.
How can you not be there?

Faith tells me you have a new "there."
Faith tells me it's a better "there."
My heart wants you back where I left you.

You were just there, two days ago.
Now, you're not.

Tuesday, May 9

I went to sleep crying and I wake up crying. I call Larry at home and there is no answer. I check at the Co-Op and he is already on his way to Jackson. Russ called. He's here, thank God. We meet at the funeral home at 9 a.m. I start crying as soon as I see him in the parking lot. My big husky brother is choked up as well. We go in and make the arrangements. My discussion and planning on Friday paved the way and saved some money. My brother is taking care of the finances for the funeral and I'll do the headstone.

I can't believe I was just here on Friday. I really thought we'd have more time. Russ takes me out to breakfast and then we go to Mom's apartment. It is still hard to open her door and not find her. It's just as hard on Russ. Aunt Ruby and Aunt Charlene arrive. So do Gwen and their sons. My nephews are big and almost grown up now. Mom was always so proud of all of her grandchildren. It meant so much to her that both Russ and I had happy marriages, homes of our own. Those are things she didn't have.

Visitation is today at 3-5 and 7-9. We go early for family viewing at 2 p.m. She just died yesterday and here we are at the funeral home. As usual everyone makes the typical comments about how good she looks. The Hospice nurse in me only sees that she is dead. I guess she does look as pretty as possible, but to me she just looks dead. They hadn't yet got her glasses or her jewelry on. I was ok until they lifted her wrist to put her watch on. Then I saw her hands and they were stiff and they truly did look dead and it hit me hard. Hands always do that to me when I go to visitations for other people. With Mom it is even harder. Russ and I and everyone else cry together.

The open visitation begins and all kinds of people come. It's amazing when you consider that the paper with the obituary just barely hit the newsstands. I guess word of mouth still travels fast. My cousin Sandy is here. I haven't seen her in years. It is good to see her and it makes my Grandma happy that she came. Many friends come from Mom's church and our old church from when we lived here. My college roommate is here. It means so much to see Marilyn. Camilla takes us all out to dinner between visitations, even Marilyn. We get a little giddy. I feel distant. I need to be back at the funeral home because that is where Mom is. Night visitation is very crowded. Mom's friends and our friends and family pack the place. The VFW ladies come and do their memorial and it is moving.

It is hard for Russ and me to see how these ladies from our childhood have aged. Mom never really looked old to me. After all, she was only 72. Plus, she never let her hair go gray, a tradition I intend to maintain! Mom and I have the same fair coloring, pale skin, blondish brown hair. We'll probably age the same. When the VFW ladies finish they lay their white carnations on the coffin one by one and we all cry. My friend Penny from high school was there. She always called Mom "Mom Pahl," and my mom really loved her. She was my maid of honor, but we've drifted apart. Still, it was wonderful to see her. I miss her. My other childhood friend, Lynn, my friend since I was four, lives in Chicago and can't come. Her mother still lives here in Jackson and she comes instead. She stands alone by the coffin for a bit before she leaves. I wonder if she's remembering when they only lived a block apart and Lynn and I literally almost lived at each other's houses. We were pretty much joined at the hip in those days of elementary school. I'd spend Friday night at her house and she'd spend Saturday night at mine. Sometimes in the summer we'd stay with each other for days. Our moms joked about it, but indulged us. Her mom was blunt and to the point, where my mother was quieter, but they both made us feel loved and secure.

Lynn and I took different paths, but we were both blessed by moms that loved us. I don't know how I go on now without that love in my life. I thank Lynn's mom for coming and give her a hug. Her eyes are moist. My friend Jenny is here. She'll be one of my rocks in the rough days ahead. Larry is here tonight without the kids. He brought the boys to the earlier visitation so that Nathan could ask his questions. Larry's also been a rock for me, very loving and supportive. It's time to go now. I'd rather just spend the night here, at the funeral home, with Mom. We stand at the coffin one more time to say goodbye. Her hand has bruises on it from those last falls. I touch her hand and it really is stiff and cold. I've touched hundreds of dead hands over the years, but it is never any less shocking. It is worse when it is my mom. It just shouldn't be.

Wednesday, May 10

Today is Mom's funeral. I can't believe I have to do this today. I get there at 9:45 a.m. for one last visitation at 10. People are already here. My friend Jan meets me in the parking lot. I needed to see her. I am so thankful she came. Mom's brother Warren is here. I haven't seen him in a few years. It's only been in recent times that he has become close again to Mom and Aunt Ruby. People even come from my old Hospice of Jackson days. It is neat that they still care.

Some of my high school friends are here as well. I am really glad that Cathie could come. She and Lynn visited my mom during her first illness, and that meant a lot to me. Some people I don't get to greet. I hope they sign the guest book.

Pastor Dave gives a beautiful message about hope. He talks about Mom's favorite Bible verse, from Psalm 118:24. He explains how "This is the day which the Lord has made." Even today is the day which the Lord has made. Pastor Dave weaves his message with

Love, Hugs, and Kisses   25

Mom's good and bad days. The same God that gave us Monday (the day she died) also gave us Palm Sunday a few weeks ago when she sang so joyfully in the Easter cantata. Pastor Dave talks about Mom's faith. He even mentions Sam's adoption. All of my friends agree it is a beautiful message, and I wish I had taped it. I do manage to snag a copy of his notes.

    At the end of the service the VFW pall bearers come up and they all salute Mom one by one. Once again we all break down in tears. Then after everyone files out we have one more family time at the coffin. I touch her one more time, and yep, it really truly is a dead hand. I don't want to leave the room, but I have to. I'd rather just keep looking at her. I'm longing for a way to stay close. When we finally do leave, they close the coffin, and the pall bearers carry her out. We are already in the family car at that point. The ride to the cemetery is tolerable, but just barely. Her grave is right by the entrance and it is open with her vault beside it as we drive by.

    At Hillcrest Cemetery they have the committal in the chapel. I like it at the graveside better. Seeing the pall bearers lift Mom's coffin out of the car and into the chapel is rough. Not much of the message in the chapel registers with me. I remember praying. Again, I don't want to leave, but I have to. We go to Mom's church and the ladies serve us a nice meal. By now I am on autopilot as I say goodbye to everyone and thank them for coming. I am aware that the day is sunny and turning hot and I long for comfortable clothes.

    Eventually we return to Mom's apartment. Relatives come back with us and it is overwhelming. Too many people in too small a space. Yet it is an empty space because Mom isn't here. She should be hosting this thing, making sure everyone has enough to drink and eat. She should be taking care of us right now. The guys begin dismantling Mom's furniture. They take her bed apart so that Larry can take the mattress in the truck. One of Russ's friends will take the frame. I want to yell at everybody to just stop, it is too soon to take Mom's life apart. But I know we have to do the heavy stuff while we have the help. I hate it. Eventually Larry heads back to Cheboygan with our boys. We agreed that since they were just at his parents' last week they need to be home now. Friends will help and the preschool will help with Sam as well for a couple of days. I'll miss them but I need to be completely free to concentrate on Mom's stuff while Russ is here to help me. We only have two days to clear out her life. Yuck.

    A bunch of us go out to dinner and I just can't deal with the commotion. My cousins head back to South Haven (two hours away) but Aunt Ruby stays to help us sort through Mom's stuff. After all, she is her only sister. Russ and Gwen and the kids go to their motel, and Aunt Ruby and I stop at Laurel's for a breather. They hit it off right away and talk art and cats. Later I take Aunt Ruby to Camilla's to spend the night, and I return to Laurel's. She babies me once again with tea and sympathy and I let her. She truly understands, as her mom died when she was eighteen.

Thursday, May 11

    I am up early, and am the first one at Mom's apartment. It is the first time I am alone since she died. I talk out loud to Mom. It helps. Camilla drops off Aunt Ruby, and then Russ and Gwen and their boys are here. In spite of the sadness it is truly wonderful to have time with Russ and his family. I've missed them all. Today turns into a very long day of sorting. Pictures, mementos, scraps of paper all are gone through. I save a few of her old grocery lists. Aunt Charlene comes and is very helpful. It diffuses some of the tension that comes with who gets what. The two aunts sort clothes. I can't bring myself to do this. Sometimes I wander away from the apartment and stroll around the other floors and into the lobby.

This senior complex used to be a luxurious hotel built in the old style. The chandeliers and the mezzanine are still here, as are the marbled stairs and lobby. It is a beautiful old building with lots of charm and nooks and crannies. I am glad Mom was so happy here for the last five years. She should have had lots more years here. Gwen makes ham sandwiches for lunch, and once again we go out for dinner. No one has yet let me pay for my own meal. I'm being spoiled rotten! After dinner Aunt Charlene goes home and Aunt Ruby goes back to Camilla's. Russ and I return to Mom's alone. It is a welcome reprieve and we set up tables to sort stuff and get organized for another long day on Friday. We bring down all of Mom's boxes from the storage room. Later I return to Laurel's and take a very long hot shower. I feel dirty with death, grungy with grief. I can't truly wash it off, but I try. I call Larry and watch ER on television with Laurel. It is a very welcome distraction. Laurel and I talk a long, long time. Again, I cry myself to sleep as I have every night since she died. *Dear Lord Jesus, help me get through this. I just don't know how to shut down Mom's life and close up her home. I still can't believe she is gone. She should still be here. Please, God, grant me your peace.*

Friday, May 12

I pick up Aunt Ruby and say goodbye to Camilla, since I won't see her again before I go home. I thank her for everything, especially for being with Mom that last night. We head to Mom's and get busy. Russ and Gwen bring donuts from Hinckley's Bakery in our childhood neighborhood. No one in the whole world can make a glazed donut like Hinckley's, and they were Mom's favorite. They bring back a bit of our childhood. The summer before my seventh grade year, as Mom recovered from her first heart attack, one of us had to be home with her all the time while Dad was at work. One of my treats during those long dull days was the early morning bike ride to Hinckley's. Since donuts were a no-no for Mom at that time, I'd buy a loaf of fresh bread for her, and sometimes a donut for me to eat on the ride back. Those were the few minutes of joy that I remember from that summer.

Today we all wolf down a couple of donuts before we get to work. We sort through boxes and pictures and papers, not really making any decisions other than who will take home what to finish sorting later. My brother and I divide the labor as equally as possible, and give Aunt Ruby a few mementos for her kids. I already gave Aunt Charlene and Aunt Pat each a cup and saucer. I give Gwen Mom's good dishes and most of the kitchen stuff, as she has never had a completed kitchen set. Mom really wanted Gwen to have the dishes, and I am glad she does. I take some of her older dishes, and jewelry and stuff.

In the afternoon I run errands with Aunt Ruby. We go to the funeral home for the copies of the death certificates that I will need to close down Mom's affairs. Then we go out to Ruth and Dale's house to say goodbye. We go up to Grandma Wahr's (Larry's grandmother) to store some of Mom's stuff in the basement, and I give Grandma one of my mom's pillows. She and Mom had always liked each other, and in this last year Grandma had called Mom nightly to check in with her. I am extremely blessed to have such wonderful in-laws. Larry's Mom and Grandma filled a very special place in my mother's life, and I am thankful. Aunt Ruby and I make a last stop at the cemetery. It hurts, but I need to see it. The grave is still mounded and fresh. Our flowers are here. I cry. My mommy has a grave and I don't want her to, so there! Aunt Ruby hugs me and lets me cry. How can my mother really be in a grave?

Later, Russ and I visit the cemetery together. We each take ribbon and some flowers to dry and save. It somehow seems important to save them. We put them in the refrigerator at Mom's apartment until we leave tomorrow. Then we meet everyone for dinner. The cousins are here to pick up Aunt Ruby so it is again a family gathering. After dinner we say goodbye to Aunt Ruby, and once again, I cry. I go back to Laurel's and keep her up late again, talking and crying. It really isn't fair since she has to get up so early for work. When I walk in the door I burst into tears in her arms. I can't cope with Mom having a grave. I don't want Mom to have a grave. I can't stand to think about her body doing the things that bodies do once they're in a grave. I hate it.

Laurel told me she also had a rough time with her mother's grave. We talk a lot about funerals and graveside services vs. chapel services. We talk about how hard it is to grasp the reality of death in physical sense, even though we are both nurses. Maybe it is worse because we are nurses. It is a long, hard night for me. I know I need sleep to drive back to Cheboygan, but I can't sleep. Tomorrow I have to leave Jackson and I'm not ready to. I have to say goodbye to Russ and I already miss him. I hate this. *Dear God, I know you are in control and I thank you for that, because I sure am not in control! I know in my head that Mom is in a better place. Help me believe it in my heart. Help me to get home somehow tomorrow.*

Saturday, May 13

It's over. Everything that can be done right now is done. I meet Russ at Mom's. First I go to Meijer's and scour the store for the stuff to preserve our flowers. It seems crucial to give some to Russ so that his flowers will make it all the way home. I can't deal with him not keeping his flowers. I get to Mom's apartment first, about 9 a.m. I finish the last of the cleaning and walk around her apartment saying goodbye. It is almost empty now. All of her furniture, most of it hand-me-downs to begin with, has been given away. The walls are empty, and her lily is gone. I gave it to the friend who gave it to her in the first place. I sit on the floor and pray. It is sunny and quiet, and I thank God that Mom had this haven for a time. I ask for strength to help me leave it.

    Russ and his family get here. I give him his flowers. We stand around eating Hinckley donuts one last time. Gwen and the kids walk out first, and Russ and I have a few last moments alone. I don't want my big brother to leave. He says he is glad I have to lock up and not him. I call him a chicken, but I agree. We hug and say our "I love yous" one more time. This is some kind of record. We had said it to each other at the funeral and now again today. Twice in one week! I don't think we had ever told each other we loved each other. We promise to do better at keeping in touch. Then he hits the road. They are going to stop in South Haven and spend more time with Aunt Ruby and the cousins. I am glad. It will be good for him to have more family time. Then I spend another 45 minutes alone. I am procrastinating. I talk out loud to Mom and I cry and I wipe out every nook and cranny, those that hadn't been done and those that had. I call Millie (her other life-long friend) to say goodbye since I hadn't done that yet. I ask both her and Camilla to stay in touch. It will be very strange not hearing regularly about Mom's best friends. I also go up and say goodbye to Bea. She became a good friend to Mom in these years at the apartment. For a brief time Uncle Bob lived here as well before he died last year. They sort of became the Three Musketeers, with Mom driving and cooking for all of them at least once or twice a week. They bickered a little, but they were devoted to each other. It drove Uncle Bob crazy that Mom would spend four dollars on fresh raspberries once a year. Mom would just say that life is too short not to have raspberries when they are in season!

    I decide to buy raspberries this summer if I find them in Cheboygan. I wait for Aunt Charlene and Aunt Pat to come and load up the rest of the stuff Russ and I just don't have room for. This breaking up of housekeeping is truly exhausting. I say one more goodbye to the aunts and then I get ready to leave. Russ forgot to take his flowers. After all that fuss. I'll take them with me and dry them and mail them to him. I walk out of Mom's apartment for the last time. Aunt Charlene has waited to walk out with me. It is awful. I'll never be back and someone else will live here. They had better appreciate it the way Mom did! We walk downstairs and I slide the keys through the slot in the office door. I get outside and hug goodbye yet again. I get in my car and watch the aunts drive off.

    I start the engine and then the terrible realization hits me. I've left both my brother's and my flowers in Mom's refrigerator! After all of that work I can't go off and leave them. I drive around the block once and then decide I absolutely have to try to retrieve them. I am obsessed. But I have no keys. My other choice is to go back to the cemetery and take the rest of the flowers from her grave. That won't be good because Russ and I already took the best ones. It is suddenly crucial that I get those flowers. Russ never had much of anything growing up and he is going to have those flowers if I have to move mountains to get them. I've always felt guilty because I had it better than he did as kids, and I can't ever make it up to him. He doesn't blame me now, but I think he did then, and I guess I always thought it was my fault. Alcoholic dad picks fights with troublesome son, and peacemaker daughter blames herself. We certainly knew our roles and filled them well.

Anyway, I park back in front of Mom's building. Ladies in the lobby recognize me and let me in. I share my problem and they try to help. We look around for the resident manager to get the master key and can't find him. I need to leave soon for Cheboygan, but I will wait forever if I have to just to get those flowers. In desperation, I peek into the slot in the office door. A miracle! Mom's keys have not fallen all the way through and I snatch them in triumph. The ladies congratulate me and I fly back to Mom's apartment. The relief is overwhelming as I open the refrigerator door and grab those blooms! I hug them and praise God. *Thank You God for being in the details, and understanding my craziness over these flowers!* I say a last goodbye, all alone to Mom, and finally feel free to leave. I cradle my flowers all the way down to the car and place them carefully on the floor. They are wrapped in wet paper towel and shaded from the sun.

I am finally ready to leave Mom's apartment, but I'm not quite ready to leave Jackson. I stop at Jay's Book Mart on the way out of town. It is another one of our old stomping grounds. One of the few things we did together as family when I was a kid was make trips to the bookstore. First to the original Jay's downtown, then to one on the west end by the highway when Mr. Jay expanded. My brother would get comic books, my mom would get magazines and maybe a paperback, and I would get a little of everything! Sometimes my dad even came with us, and he would pick up a bestseller. Now the sign for Jay's beckons and I can't resist. Immediately inside the store two books jump off the racks at me. One is *Motherless Daughters* which I have already seen at Laurel's. I don't want to be a motherless daughter, but I guess if I'm going to be one, I'd better read up on it! The other book that I seem to need is called *From Beginning to End* by Robert Fulghum. It is about the rituals of our lives. Maybe it will be comforting as I leave the ritual of Mom's funeral and try to figure out what in the world I am going to do now. At the counter, the sales lady is kind and comments on my book choices. I end up spilling my story, telling her about Mom's death and the need to come to Jay's one more time. She shares that she lost her mother a few years before and tells me some of her story. I ask if it ever gets better and she just says, "It gets different." We both have tears in our eyes as I leave. *Thank You Lord, for putting her behind that counter today, just when I need her. Maybe now I can actually leave town.* As my roommate and I used to say, "Let's blow this pop stand!"

    This time I actually do drive for more than five minutes. I drive all the way to Cheboygan. I think I have car trouble once, but the kindly gas station attendant tells me I just over-filled the oil somehow. *Thank You, God, for traveling mercies.* I couldn't have dealt with a major car problem right now. I get home around five or six. I never want to leave again. I go to the phone automatically to call Mom and tell her I am home safe. Then I remember. I whisper it to her instead. Then I call Ruth and let her know I'm home in one piece, and it helps a little to hear her voice. Seeing my guys helps too. We have pizza for supper. It is all I can manage. Adrenaline finally runs out and exhaustion hits. Tomorrow is Mother's Day. What lousy timing. I don't know how I'll get through church. *Help me begin this part of my life, Lord.* The funeral is over and now I'm just left with missing her. I'd rather be back at the funeral than at this stage. This feels lonely and never ending. I've always been fascinated with stages of life, both the kind that you act on and pass through. I even wrote about them in college and high school. Now I'm in a stage I really don't want to be in. I hope there are intermissions. *Help me, Lord!*

2. Disconnected

Sunday, May 14

    Mother's Day is ok at first. Pastor calls early to tell me what he will be saying at church about Mom's Day. He is just preparing me, and that is kind, but I cry anyway. Having my own kids at this point helps. I remember all of those other infertile Mother's Days before adoption made us a family. On those Sundays I celebrated my own mom but grieved not having children. Today I will celebrate my own children but I'll grieve not having Mom. I guess you can't win them all! In church I receive a flower. Afterwards, we go to McDonald's for lunch. I am too tired to cook, and the budget is tight after all of this travel. At home we all take naps. I sleep heavy with dreams about giving away Mom's things.

    I wake up when my dad calls. This is the second time I've talked to him this week. It is hard but good to hear his voice. Since I've had children we've gradually been making peace with one another. The fact that he has been sober for ten years helps a lot. He seems happily married to Jane, and I am glad that he isn't alone in Texas. He is also genuinely sad about Mom. After all, they were married 32 years. I don't think it was ever a lack of caring that broke them up. It was just the alcohol and all the assorted crud that goes along with it. Anyway, it is good to talk to Dad. He is sincere. I cry again. He tells me he loves me and that he'll try to send some money toward Mom's grave marker. He wants to do something for us. He understands a little bit about how big this is for me. He remembers how close I was to Mom as a kid. He says he'll also call Russ today. I hope he does. I think that they are also finding their way back together. Russ is still bitter, but I think he wants to heal. It really bothered him that Mom and Dad made such a mess of their finances. It hurt him that Mom had nothing at her time of death. He vowed that he would never do that to his children, and he told me he has life insurance in place. We do too. We'll never be rich, but our kids shouldn't have to worry about paying for our funerals.

  I talk with Dad about thirty minutes. He tells me that Jane is confused by the Pahl family. We are a strange bunch, I guess. We never meet a stranger and once you're a part of the family, you're always a part of the family, unless you choose not to be. It baffles her that Dad and Mom could be divorced and yet Mom is still a daughter and a sister to all of the Pahls. It's just the way we are, and it makes sense to us even if it doesn't to anyone else. When I hang up I cry some more and Larry hugs me.

  I am haunted by a week ago. A week ago today was Mom's last day on earth. I feel like somehow I should have known. I talked to her on the phone. I worried about moving her to foster care. I made plans. She was getting worse, but I didn't think she was dying right then. I would have been there if I had known. Tomorrow when I wake up it will be exactly a week since her death. Time of death on the death certificate is listed as 6:35 a.m. when the nurse found her, but I know it was earlier. I believe she died between 3 and 4 a.m. when I was praying for her. I don't want it to be a week since she died. Oh, Mom, I already miss you so much. I want good times back. I want you healthy. I want Nathan when he was two years old getting off the elevator on your floor and running down the hall to find Grandma. Sammy was just learning how to do that when you died. He'll never get the chance to "go find Grandma." Mom, I want you to see the boys grow up. I want four generation pictures with you in them. I hate this grief thing! It doesn't help when I know so much about it from my Hospice training. I wish I'd never taken all of those classes in grief and bereavement. It's kind of hard to stay in denial when my mind is saying, "Oh yeah, this is denial!"

Monday, May 15

Well, it's official. It is nighttime and I have survived the first week without Mom. Exhaustion and fatigue have hit with a heavy hand. Bonnie, who has had more death in her life than any one woman should (a son, a husband, a mother-in-law, a brother), warned me about this. She said, "Be careful about sleeping too much. It can be depression." If anyone should know, she should. I'm not going to get too worried about myself just yet. After all, I am depressed and tired, but I think it's normal. In the middle of all of this I am still a mom of two very active young boys. I am awake when they are, which seems like all of the time. I lay on the couch when Sam does nap, and I let Nathan watch TV. Today I cared for Sam while Nathan was at preschool, fed and changed Sam, dozed twice, unpacked enough of the car so that I could go pick Nathan up, went to the bank, cooked supper, did dishes, and bathed and good-nighted each kid. I talked coherently to Larry, and also on the phone to Jenny and Paula and Bonnie and Russ and Aunt Charlene and others who called. I think that's pretty good for fresh grief!

The hardest time today was when I started unloading the car. I dropped some trash, it spilled all over, and I threw a temper tantrum.

I didn't lie on the garage floor and kick and scream, but only because there was oil on the floor. I did yell and cry and stomp my feet. Good thing I was inside the garage where no one could see. Then today at five, when I would normally call Mom to see how her weekend went, I felt lost. I tried to call her anyway. I got the automatic recorded, "This number has been disconnected" message, and somehow it made me feel better. We are disconnected, Mom and I, and the recorded message on the other end of the line validates that fact. *Dear God, will I ever feel connected again? I thank you that I am connected to You, through Jesus Christ.*

Tuesday, May 16

It is only Tuesday. It should be next year. I hate grief. I miss Mom. This coming weekend is the women's retreat on Mackinac Island. I went to it a year ago and Mom drove up here and stayed with the kids. We spent time together both before and after the retreat. We had a great time. She did all of my laundry, as she always did when she stayed with us. It amazed me, as usual. Somehow the concept of being caught up on laundry is one that she gets and one that totally baffles me. The only time I'm ever caught up is when Mom stays with us. Oops. Present tense is speaking again. I have to get used to thinking in the past tense. Anyway, that week with Mom was truly wonderful. We enjoyed the kids, cooked together, laughed together. I begged her to stay an extra day, and she did. When she finally left I cried as I waved goodbye. I was hit with the fear that she would never return to my home. I remember being upset because I was getting a new sofa the next day and she wouldn't see it. A month later Mom got sick for the first time with congestive heart failure and she never did come back. She never saw that couch. I'll probably never be caught up on laundry again.

Another hard moment struck today while I was rocking Sammy. He won't have any memories of Mom, and I don't know if I'll be able to make her seem real to him. I rearranged furniture today. Right now it helps to keep busy. Moving furniture has always been cheaper than therapy, anyway! My husband can always tell when I'm upset when he comes home and trips over the couch in a new and strange place. Today I turned the closet under the stairs into a little playroom for the kids. It is a small, cozy nook and they like it. Mom's mail started arriving here today. So far just sympathy cards addressed to her family at her old address. There was even an anonymous gift of cash. *Thank you, Lord for the kindness of people who care so much about us.* It is almost bedtime now. I have survived another day.

Wednesday, May 17

I hate being so sad and tired all of the time. I know this is just the beginning, and I have to let myself grieve. I'd really rather not. I'm ready to stop grieving, right now, done, finished. Today I keep thinking of last Wednesday, about Mom's funeral. In some ways I'd rather be back there than here. I call AARP today and cancel Mom's insurance. That is my major Mom task for the day. I take care of the kids and cook dinner. I run to the store for milk and reach into my pocket. I find Mom's grocery list. It is the last one she wrote, the one I filled for her before I left Jackson for Cheboygan, just before she died. I sit in the parking lot and cry. I forget the milk and go home. I keep the list. Nathan tells me at bedtime that we should know Grandma's phone number in heaven and call her and say goodnight. I agree. I tell him to pray and to ask God to give her his message. I don't know if that was theologically correct, but at this point it comforts a five-year-old and that five-year-old's mommy!

Today I also called Toni. Her adult daughter died two weeks before Mom, and she is in the midst of a terrible, very different kind of grief. It is still comforting to talk to each other. I also called Grandma and told her that I loved her. I know she never expected to outlive my Mom, and that this has been hard for her. Even though Mom was a daughter-in-law, she was much more than that to Grandma. Now that it is bedtime I can't sleep. I have decisions to make about child care if I go back to work part-time and when to return to leading Bible study. Every decision seems major right now. I want my Mommy!

Thursday, May 18

It is a black morning. I am tired and grumpy. I can't cope. I call Bonnie and we go to lunch. It helps. Then she comes back to the house and sits with me as I unpack a few of my Mom's things. When I get the mail, I find a picture that Dad sent. It is a four-generation photo taken when he was a child. He must be sorting stuff, too. I have to figure out Mom's remaining bills. I call the phone company and get that settled. Mom didn't leave any money, so any donations that come in we'll use for her grave marker.

I go through Mom's purse today. It still smells like her. Her lipstick and powder feel comforting, familiar. I know Mom had many different purses in the course of her life, yet they always looked the same to me. Either black or navy blue, they were always large with two or three different sections. My mother always called it her "pocketbook." In my childhood it contained plastic rain bonnets, a foldable plastic drinking cup that I thought was magical, and pennies for the gumball machines. That purse always occupied the same place every night of her life. It would rest beside her bed, next to her silver metal flashlight, whether she was at home or away visiting someone. I used to tease her about being such a creature of habit, and she replied, "I like to be prepared." One time when she and Aunt Ruby visited me in Cheboygan, I was lamenting the lack of an extension cord to hook up a reading lamp in the guest bedroom. My ever-prepared mother piped up with, "I have one," and proceeded to pull it out of her commodious pocketbook! Aunt Ruby and I got so tickled about that. We laughed and laughed. I will keep my mother's purse forever. Someday someone will go through my things and find it and wonder why. I also have one blanket from Mom's laundry that still smells like her.

Friday, May 19

I cannot get over this awful fatigue. Maybe I'll sleep better tonight. Last night I had a horrible nightmare. The phone was ringing and I couldn't get to it in time. I woke Larry up and was hysterical. I was sure it was bad news about Mom. The night before I talked in my sleep to Aunt Ruby about Mom. Poor Larry. It is a good thing not much disturbs his rest. Today I feel disconnected to people. Some well-meaning folks call, but I can tell they don't really understand. At the store they are selling VFW buddy poppies and it reminds me of Mom and her involvement with those sales in Jackson. Mom's new checks come today in the mail. I ordered them that last week of her life. I can't bring myself to throw them out. They have her name on them. That matters, somehow. I put them with the other things I can't pitch.

No sympathy cards came today, a first since she died. I hope a few more trickle in. They help. They remind me that others are still aware of Mom as a person, of our grief. I manage a little housework and bill paying today. I have to function at least a little bit every day. *Dear Jesus, help me feel more connected to those around me. Please keep those sympathy cards coming. They really do help.*

Sunday, May 21

Tomorrow will be two weeks since Mom died. Two weeks ago my life changed forever, but the world goes on. I want to scream "stop!" Two weeks ago, funeral week, I was cocooned. Now I'm not. It will probably be a long time before I see Mom again in heaven. Today I want to call her to tell her about my Sunday dinner. We loved cooking and sharing our menus with each other. I get my love of all of that from her. Just like her, I enjoy trying new recipes and changing them to my tastes. I want to tell Mom about today's London Broil and how good and satisfying it is. I want to tell her about Nathan's strawberry cake for celebrating Adoption Day. I want to reminisce with her about bringing Nathan home five years ago on the 18th and finalizing his adoption four years ago on the 24th. I am so thankful that she knew Sam's adoption was final. I remember that Grandma Lockwood died the week we finalized Nathan's adoption and how glad I was that she had known about Nathan for a year before she died. At least Mom knew Sam for fifteen months. I'm not thrilled with this combination of finalizing adoptions and going to funerals. I would prefer to keep my joy and my grief separate. I guess life doesn't work that way. Maybe that's a good thing.

There were times this weekend when the pain wasn't as sharp, but right now it is raw and burning. It is a physical longing for my mother's comfort. Who would I most like to talk to about Mom's death? My mother, of course. I guess this journal is one way of trying to do that. Lately I've been trying to suppress the tears when people are around. Old habits come back to haunt me from my childhood when it wasn't safe to cry. The first week of my grief I could cry around people, but now I don't feel safe anymore. At the cemetery Russ fought to hold back his tears because "she never cried." We talked about how we never saw Mom cry other than maybe a trickle down her cheek at funerals. I told Russ it is ok to cry. Nathan and Sam have both seen me cry. I hope they grow up with a healthy attitude about tears.

Monday, May 22

Happy Anniversary to Larry and Me. Each day seems like the hardest. Today there is no anniversary card from Mom and there never will be again. She never forgot my anniversary, and I know she wouldn't have this year, even as sick as she was. Mom signed her cards and letters, "Love, hugs, and kisses, Mom." I should have saved more of those. Thank God I have a few left. I still feel shocked that Mom isn't here. I want to hear her voice on the phone one more time. Last night I dreamed again about getting a call about her dying. The anxiety and fear of phone calls bearing bad news traumatized me more than I realized. It is complicated by the old childhood fears of "bad news" phone calls. I don't know that we got so very many bad phone calls late at night when I was a kid, but evidently the ones I remember left their mark. I take the flowers from Mom's grave out of the silicone powder today. Most of them have dried well, except for the daisies. Now I just have to send them to Russ. It seems a little silly to hang onto funeral flowers, but I handle each one gently and tenderly, like a precious treasure. A little thing and a big thing combined. A tangible way to grieve and it helps keep me sane.

Tuesday, May 23

I'm mad today. I can't find two old friends to tell them about Mom. They both live out of state and have moved around and have sort of lost touch. Yet they were there for me at important times and they should know about Mom. I need them to know. I've been there for both of them when they lost a parent, and I need them now. I can't find a phone number so I sent a card to their last known address. Maybe I'll get lucky. *Please, Lord, help me get an acknowledgment from them.* Today I actually put the dried flowers in a box, wrap it and get it ready to mail to Russ. I also settle one more bill for Mom. I take care of a sick Nathan and a well Sammy and cook supper and do housework and cry some more and decide I am too tired and sad and I don't like it! My nightmares last night were about large, ugly spiders. Today I manage a nap and dream that we know Mom is dying and I'm trying to arrange for Hospice and they are taking pictures of Mom and her apartment building. I still haven't had a comforting Mom dream. I hope I do.

Wednesday, May 24

Two weeks ago was Mom's funeral. Today I begin the thank you notes. Bonnie thinks I may be having nightmares because these notes are hanging over my head. I think I'd be having bad dreams anyway, but maybe she's right. Regardless, the notes need to be done. I complete four of them today. Last night's dream took place at Burden's, the funeral home in Jackson that we always use. We were at someone's funeral other than my Mom's, but all of the same people were there. Mom wasn't. Larry was working there to make extra money and he told me he was going to change jobs and go into the funeral home business. Very strange!

Nathan has tonsillitis. Sam has wheezes. I sure will be glad when everyone is well. Today I walk by Mom's picture and stop and stare. I think, "She isn't really gone, not really dead." The enormity of missing her is still beyond my comprehension. Every day there are little reminders of who she was to me and my children. I want to call her and say I like the way her mini chopper works, one of the kitchen items that I brought home from her apartment. I know she'd be glad I'm making good use of it.

    P.S. Dear Mom, tonight was one of those suppers when you would have said, "Oh, why do we have to get full so fast?" We all would have laughed and teased you because you've been saying that at every good meal for as long as I can remember. Tonight's meal was simple home cooking with scalloped potatoes, sloppy joes and broccoli. If you had made it you would have said, "That was good, even if I did make it myself!" Another Mom-ism that I would love to hear again!

Thursday, May 25

    Today is the best day I've had. It is almost a good day. Lots of emotional support. Bible study this morning, a sympathy card in the mail from Laurie, a call from Toni, and a call from Laurel. Today I manage some more paperwork for doctor bills and health insurance. I have a hard time making myself do these chores, but once I do them I feel better. I didn't get any more thank you cards done, but I organized all of the sympathy cards. Last night's dream was just a jumble of people and images from the funeral. At one point we were in a horrible foster care home where we were considering placing Mom. My college roommate was there. An old man died and I was struck by the grief of his only friend. So far today, no tears. If I make it through the whole day, it will be the first day since before Mom died that I haven't cried. The kindness of strangers is amazing. In canceling two of Mom's accounts, both people were so sympathetic on the other end of the phone that I felt like I had made a friend. It all helps. *Dear Lord, thank you for kind voices. I also thank you that I never actually had to move Mom out of her home. It would have killed her.*

Friday, May 26

There have been unexpected gifts in this valley of grief. One is the urgency to write. I can't not write about Mom and this process. I don't have to struggle for words or motivation. For a writer, that is truly a gift! Another gift is the new closeness with my brother. He called today and we talked for thirty minutes. He has been sick with strep, pneumonia, and an eye infection. He is on meds and doing better now. He has been busy laminating things from Mom's scrapbook that he wants to save.

Mom and Dad were both very active in the VFW, and at one point Mom was the state president of the auxiliary. I used to joke about her being the great high mucky muck, but it really was a big deal. She had a wonderful scrapbook from her year as president, and that is what Russ is wading through now. Russ is even talking about going to visit Dad. I hope he does. They have such a troubled past. Dad's drinking and Russ' rebellion were a terrible combination. There was violence and ugliness and estrangement. Gradually, though, I have hope that they will find their way back to each other. Russ has certainly turned his life around. He has a terrific career, a wonderful wife and kids. Mom was so very proud of him. Last night's dream was about Mom again. This time she had breast cancer and was having a mastectomy. I was witnessing it in all of its gory mess. I told Russ that I was having a lot of weird dreams. I told him that I woke Larry up to chase the spiders away one night, and Russ said, "You're married to a strong man." I guess you have to be strong to be married to me!

Yesterday really was the first day I didn't cry. I wonder if I am all cried out. Today I order a big geranium for Mom's grave, courtesy of Aunt Ruby. Ruth went by the grave and said it is flat now

Love, Hugs, and Kisses **47**

and seeded with grass. It is convenient having my sister-in-law Judy as a florist. Her business is right next to the farm, and Ruth works for her. All I have to do is call them, and they take care of the flowers for Mom's grave. I really need to get her marker on it. Ruth and I had a good talk today. We both wondered which way Mom's head is facing. It shouldn't matter, but it does. There is still something so awful about my mother being in a box in a hole in the ground. A coffin and a grave happens to someone else--not to Mom! I know she isn't really there and that her body is just a shell, but it still bugs me. If I let myself dwell on it, I get into really creepy emotional trouble.

    If I start thinking about body decay, I really lose it. Maybe that is why I am having nightmares. I keep thinking about that ghoulish song from childhood that my brother delighted in teaching me: "Never laugh when a hearse goes by, for you will be the next to die... they bury you down about six feet deep... the worms crawl in, the worms crawl out, the ants play pinochle on your snout...."

    Thanks, Russ for establishing that song so firmly in my brain! Do other people have these thoughts? I'll be glad when years have gone by and I can know that there is nothing left but nice clean bones instead of any part of a body that resembles my mother in any way. Time for tears. Big time. Nathan just brought me tulips. He wasn't supposed to pick them but he didn't know that. A love offering from my child that I will treasure. *Dear Lord, help me deal with the gruesome thoughts that keep haunting me about Mom's body. I know these thoughts are not from you. Bind them and get rid of them in the name of Jesus, please.* Death is gruesome. No wonder satan likes it. *Thank You God, for defeating death through Jesus Christ my Lord.*

    I had better call someone or I'll go nuts. I call Laurel. What a Godsend and a treasure. She understands immediately and says she went through the same thing. I ask her if she is just saying that to make me feel better, and she assures me she isn't. She told me that Mom's body probably isn't even recognizable anymore. I don't know if she is right but I don't care because it makes me feel better. We talk about death not being like the formaldehyde cadavers in anatomy lab. She tells me how God designed nature to quickly reclaim its own, using the analogy of vines invading a house if left unattended. She even makes me laugh. Two weeks after her mother died she went through a stage where she couldn't be intimate because her mother would see her. We got to laughing about how, of course, our mothers never, ever had intimate relations except for when they got pregnant, and they did that with their clothes on and in the dark!

    I feel so much better. Laurel and I agree that no one else's death will hit me just like this. We are now both part of a club we didn't want to join. Laurel says that it is a new dimension that will forever change me. *Thank You God, for Laurel, for my rocking chair, for the sunshine of today, for my journal, and for the telephone. All are tangible comforts in the middle of pain.*

    P.S. Laurel also told me these thoughts are probably more of a torment about my mom than they would be about anyone else because our mothers are our first comforter and snuggler, our first touch. She is right.

3. I Finally Unpack

Saturday, May 27

Grief is changing me. I alternate between total exhaustion and frenzied fits of activity. Heaven forbid, I'm taking my first steps toward being a morning person! I find myself doing things like cleaning the bathroom and washing dishes before 9:00 a.m. I am writing and reading in my Bible in the mornings. What a change. I wonder if it will last? After all, I am the classic night owl. Just like my dad, I fall asleep at one or two in the morning, and feel best if I can sleep in until nine or ten. Unfortunately with kids, that just doesn't work. Since the children came, morning for me has been a time to be dragged through, looking forward to the moment when I can doze on the couch! Before kids, when I worked full time, I first took a 3-11 shift. Then I worked two or three jobs with normal business hours, from 8-5. Much more reasonable than the daytime nursing shift of 7-3. Even with reasonable daytime hours I still felt tired all of the time!

Last night my dreams were again a jumble about Mom's death, with friends comforting me. My dreams seem to be getting less specific. I wonder if they will fade altogether with time. This body thing that Laurel and I talked about yesterday is still bugging me. Even though we've been separated by miles, this permanent physical separation by death is devastating. The fact that Mom's body can actually be "amouldering in the grave" (like John Brown's from the song) is shocking and gruesome. I do not approve! I know Mom will have a new heavenly body and that her soul is safe and happy. Mom's faith in Jesus and her belief in heaven are a comfort now. However, right now I still have to deal with her earthly body and my own earthly fears and frights. At least talking to Laurel seemed to have forestalled gruesome nightmares last night.

    I get a bill from the pharmacy today. It is addressed "to the estate of..." That's a crummy address, isn't it. Well, Mom, apparently the billing people know that you're dead. I had stopped in there during the week of your funeral and I thought this was all settled. I guess I'll have to call them. I hate these details. I am not a detail person by nature, and stuff like this really weighs on me. Mom, I know that it is too soon to understand all of the ways in which I've lost you. Today, it seems that every aspect of my life feels your absence. When I do laundry, I picture you here folding my clothes. When I'm with the kids, I see you as the doting grandmother. When I cook, I imagine sharing menus and food with you. I can't stop missing you. Thursday the tears wouldn't come, today they won't stop. I want you back.

Sunday, May 28

    Church today was worshipful. I cried during "Amazing Grace." I remember buying our first stereo when we lived on Morrell Street in Jackson. We also bought three 45s to play. We went home and played "Amazing Grace" by Judy Collins over and over. It was your favorite. We also bought "Tie a Yellow Ribbon" by Tony Orlando and Dawn, and "The Lion Sleeps Tonight." Hearing that hymn today brought back good memories of singing in the sunroom

Love, Hugs, and Kisses **51**

to our new records, with me pretending the broom was a microphone. There were happy moments in that house on Morrell Street. Before Dad's drinking got worse, before Russ got in trouble the first time, before your first heart attack. I used to tell myself I had a normal childhood. There were moments that qualified for that distinction! The stereo and the sunroom provided a lot of those times. I was talking with Larry today about a normal family, and how we are models of that to some that we know who aren't in such a situation. He said, "Why do we have to take on that role?" I told him, "It's a blessing. Count it!" That would make a good bumper sticker, or a t-shirt slogan, wouldn't it? Positive and to the point! Grief has the ability to focus a light on my blessings. With Mom gone, the people that remain in my life are even more precious. They truly are blessings, and I'm counting all of them!

Today, we clear the Dairy Queen hurdle. We attend a graduation party, and then spontaneously, while my courage is running high, I take Nathan for ice cream. Dairy Queen was his place to take Grandma. Every time she visited, if it was open, he "took Grandma" to lunch. They would share onion rings and ice cream, and have a grand old time. Sometimes I got invited, sometimes not. Today Nathan asks to go home before he even finishes his ice cream. This is Grandma's place, and she isn't here. Yesterday, Nathan had a bout of rage. It went on and on. I think he just doesn't really understand why we can't see Grandma anymore. He is also tired from being sick this week. I finally ended the whole thing by getting silly once he was in his bath. I put toothpaste on his dirty toe and fingernails and started brushing them with a toothbrush. He thought that was great fun, and was all right after that. *Dear Lord, please give me the strength to meet the needs of my family. Help me help Nathan with his feelings. Please keep the cards and phone calls coming just a little longer. They help so much.*

Monday, May 29

    Memorial Day. Flags, parades, and speeches. VFW ladies in blue hats march just like Mom used to. Memorial Day speeches make me cry. "Taps" makes me cry. I remember attending Memorial Day parades in Jackson with my friend Lynn. Watching my parents march by, we would travel as much of the parade route as we could along the crowded sidewalks. Sometimes there would be a picnic afterwards. Is every single event this year going to affect me this way? Probably. I should just be expecting it, but it still surprises me. Last night I dreamed I had breast cancer and VFW people were helping me to find treatment. When I woke up, my right breast was throbbing. Today is the three-week mark of Mom's death. It feels more like three years.

Tuesday, May 30

    Last night was the worst yet. I cried gut-wrenching tears in bed. My chest and stomach ached afterwards. Today I take the kids to the playground. I am craving sunshine. Jan and Jeanie call when I get home. Thank You, Lord. Jeanie and I talk about grief and funerals. We both think that cremation can complicate grief if there isn't a viewing of the body. After all, in our neighborhoods we burn our leaves, our trash. I couldn't have dealt with burning Mom's body. I know it is ok for some people. To some, cremation is purifying and freeing. Just not for me. Jeanie had trouble with a cremation of a relative, and I commiserate.

Wednesday, May 31

    Today four things come in the mail for Mom. Two are bills,

one is a receipt, and one is her new medicaid card. She's dead, and she gets more mail than I do! I'll be glad when the bill part is over. I hate that the most. Today I take Bonnie to lunch and the kids to the park. Being outside helps. The sunshine warms a dark and cold spot inside me. I have more phone calls from friends when I get home. Marilyn calls and it is good to talk to my college roomie. I talk to another friend for an hour and a half. Today is a tearless day until dinnertime. I want to hear Mom's voice. I cope and get the dishes done.

  Tomorrow it will be June. The month my Mom died will be over. It will be easier for other people to forget. Time is standing still for me. I am frozen in this place. I do what I have to do to get through each day, but sometimes it hurts worse than the day Mom died. I hadn't discovered all of the ways I would miss Mom at that point. Time will just keep on passing, and it will be longer and longer since I talked to her, and soon I will forget the sound of her voice. I know I will hear her voice in heaven, but that seems far away.

  There is a grim determination about my faith right now. It isn't lost or shaken, but I dislike this path my life is taking. I trust God to get me through this. Christ is my solid rock, but I'm not standing on it right now. Instead, I am laying prostrate on my rock with my arms clinging tightly. There is no joy on this rock, but there is a strength. I trust that the joy will come back someday. Faith doesn't eliminate grief, it illuminates it. In the darkest of my nights, I feel lonely, but I know that I am not alone. This is grace, this is mercy, this is comfort.

Thursday, June 1
  Bible study today is good. Later, I take the kids to the playground. There is a mom and her adult daughter and two

grandchildren playing together. They are about my kids' ages, and they have fun. I talk a little with the mom and daughter. It is bittersweet. I'll never have those shared moments with Mom again. I want to tell these people to treasure this day, to store it up against the future. I keep my mouth shut. I don't want to be carted off to the loony bin just yet. Tonight I call Aunt Ruby. Her voice is the closest to Mom's that I can get. It helps. *Dear Lord, thank you for people like Aunt Ruby who truly miss my mom. It reminds me that I am not alone.*

Friday, June 2

Nathan, my first baby, graduates from preschool today. The first milestone that Mom misses. Nathan is just as serious as a Ph.D. scholar! The kids walk up an aisle and receive a diploma, a carnation and a hug from Miss Michele. I cry. I sit next to another preschool parent, my occasional hairdresser. She did Mom's hair every time Mom visited. My mother was of that generation of women who got their hair done every week, and no little trip to Cheboygan would ever interfere with that. Lori always did a super job on Mom's very fine and thinning hair. She even backcombed it to Mom's satisfaction. She shares sympathy and a hug with me today. She hadn't yet heard about Mom's death and it is a relief to tell her.

Later today we go on a garage sale trek. We need a treat after graduation. I find a five-dollar bike with an infant seat for Sam, and a new helmet for Nathan. As soon as he's a little steadier, we'll be off. The outdoors is a balm and a comfort these days. I've never really been bothered by the weather before, but lately, gloomy days really irritate me. I have to be outside every day right now. I think God designed sunshine partially for grief-stricken folks like me. I put it on my list of things to thank Him for now, and again when I get to heaven. Other good things happen today. I finally get a card from my long lost friend that I was so ticked at not being able to find. I found one friend, never did hear from the other. The glass is half full, not half empty. My friend writes a comforting note, and I thank God for this answer to prayer.

Saturday, June 3

I'm in a snit, a hissy tizzy fit, a full-blown icky yucky snit! I'm tired, I'm tired of taking care of everyone, and I am tired of grieving. In five days it will be a month since Mom died. That's lousy. If I can't have her back I want to go back to the week she died. Then grieving came easily and I was surrounded by other people grieving. Now it feels like, "Ok, it is almost a month, so let's get on with life." I can't. I see Peggy today. Her parents have both died. She tells me how it changed her life forever and how she just wanted time to stop. It stood still for her while everyone else just carries on. I agree. I don't want my life to have changed forever. I liked it just fine the way it was. I'm always busy, I'm almost always surrounded by someone, but I am lonely. This is Larry's busiest time of year. He is supportive, but working long hours. This isn't just grief, this is a pity party. My "sorts" are completely out and my "gruntle" is as "dissed" as it can be.

Sunday, June 4

Columnist Bob Talbert of the Detroit *Free Press* has a concept involving "stupid time" vs. "silly time." Stupid time can be time spent on hold, silly time is time playing with the kids on the lawn. Each time can be the same amount of minutes, but they feel like they are in different dimensions, passing by differently. I now add "grief time" vs. "joy time" to his contrasts. In grief time, no time is passing, and then it is a month since the death occurred. It is impossible that a month has passed because it was just now that the bad news hit. I am living in grief time. Joy time has to be out there waiting for me. It must be.

Monday, June 5
>Soul Solace: A bike ride to the beach.
>Waves pounding as wind blows.
>Bible study with ladies who want to learn.
>This journal.
>Summer porch-sitting in my freshly painted wicker chair.
>Watching my kids be kids. Helping them be kids.
>Cleaning out the gunk. Corners, closets, cupboards.
>My kitchen rocker.
>Losing weight.
>Pretty earrings and good perfume.
>A good mystery from the library.
>Friends who aren't tired of me yet.
>Hot tea with cream in my favorite mug.
>Homemade shortbread.
>Hard work.
>Rest.

Mom, I hope heaven allows you to hear and see me. Yet, maybe not. You would be sad because I am so sad. The Bible says there are no tears in heaven. Yet I believe you have some sense of me, yet without feeling the grief I feel. I know you are joyful in heaven. I hope I find some more of your letters. They are a special gift right

Love, Hugs, and Kisses

now, especially the "Dear Karen," opening and the "love, hugs, and kisses" ending. I wish I had saved every letter from my college years and our years in Cheboygan. At least I have some. Dear Lord, I think I need to talk to my dad soon. For the first time in my adult life I am craving a daddy hug. I guess I just want a parent and he is all I have left. I remember the walks and talks he and I used to have before his drinking got worse and he fell forever off that pedestal I had him on. I know now we could have a healthy hug. Dear Lord, please let him come to know You. Amen.

Wednesday, June 6

    1:15 a.m. I am too tired and wound up from yesterday. I bit off more than I could chew. I baby-sat for some neighborhood kids and at one point I had six kids on my porch. I shouldn't have said yes. I don't like caring for other peoples' kids even under the best of circumstances! Three friends come by and I cook an extra meal for someone who is sick. Then Larry comes home and tells me he has been asked to interview in a town far away from here for a job. It is next week and I am invited to go with him. We'll stay in a bed-and-breakfast at their expense and have a night away from the kids. I really don't want to move, but if it is a better opportunity for Larry, I am willing to go. The kids aren't in school yet, so it would be easier now than later. If it happens, maybe we could have a sunnier house. I really like this house, but not the dark living room.

    I talk to my mother-in-law tonight. She and Grandma went to Mom's grave today and the geranium is planted. Someone else planted more red and white ones and the VFW marker and flag is there. It helps to know that. Mom would be so pleased that people are being so thoughtful. Ruth said that the church put a letter on the bulletin board from Mom. She wrote it for the church's fiftieth anniversary and my sister-in-law Nancy is going to get a copy for me. That would make Mom happy. Time for tears. I postponed them all day and that is not a good idea.

Wednesday, June 7-later
One year ago today Mom got sick for the first time. I wasn't ready to lose her then and I'm not ready now. I keep thinking of things I need to ask Mom, things only she would know. Does she remember when our baby-sitter Millie worked her last day and I was so sick from grief? Who are all of those people in her nursing pictures? When did she decide to be a nurse? The list goes on and on. Conversations I still need to have. I am blessed. I know she loved me. I know she was proud of me. She knew I loved her.

Thursday, June 8
One month. *Thank You, Lord. You are getting me though today.* Anticipating it was worse than the actual day. Dad calls. He is in the "good dad" mode and it helps. No criticism, just nice conversation. He doesn't ask me even once about my weight! While we talk I am filled with longing to see him. It is out of the question financially right now. *Please, Lord, if it is necessary for healing, please make it possible for me to see him before he dies. Thank You!* I call Russ and Aunt Charlene calls. Jan calls and we find laughter. I tell her about my "It's a blessing. Count it!" motto for tee shirts and we get giddy. We agree that for certain full-figured women, wearing that tee shirt could be a problem. We disintegrate into tacky jokes and it is all downhill from there. We finally decide a refrigerator magnet would be a better choice! *It feels wonderful to laugh. Thank You, God.* Aunt Charlene tells me she is going to church with Grandma once or twice a month. She isn't sure why, but says it feels

good. I am glad for her. I always pray for her.
    When I talk with Russ I tell him that today is a month since Mom died. He says, "It isn't the eighth already, is it?" I am so relieved that he knows Mom died on the eighth. That little detail is important. Russ agrees that it seems both longer and shorter since Mom died. That weird time dimension thing again. Tonight I visit the library with Nathan. Mom used to take me to the library when I was a kid, so this is a soul solace. I cling to these solaces these days. Mom, I love you. If you can see or hear me, if God thinks it best, please see me in a dream and be there with your presence. I hear that happens to other people, why not to me? But whatever God thinks is best is ok with me.

Friday, June 9
    Today is ok. Sam hugs his stuffed Barney toy and I have a flashback to Nathan at that age, with Mom at Christmas. Barney was a favorite right then, and Nathan had Barney pjs and slippers and his huggable Barney. Mom won't be with us for any more Christmases. She won't know Sam. So much for an ok day.

Saturday, June 10
    I had horrible, screaming nightmares last night. I dreamed the tub was overflowing and I couldn't save Sammy in time. I pulled him out and started CPR and woke up. *Please God, make me less paranoid about losing everyone I love! Please protect everyone I love!*

Sunday, June 11
    Today is a too busy Sunday. I have started taking on the occasional Hospice visit because we need the money, but it is hard. I

see one patient before church and one after church. I spend church in the nursery with Sam. Not exactly worshipful. Nathan gets a cut lip today when an older kid roughhouses. The house is messy, but I manage to cook a good dinner. Laura stops by and I provide a listening ear. After Nathan goes to bed I get out my weights and exercise. Who would have thought that the Couch Potato Queen would find solace in exercise? It works, and I am losing weight as well. Before bed, I wash dishes and throw in a load of laundry. Last night's dream was me wandering around Mom's apartment building. Mom wasn't there and I knew that someone else was living in her apartment. I chase up and down in elevators and on the stairs but never find Mom.

      I wake up this morning missing her more than ever. I really wish there was someone I could ask to tell me how I am doing in all of this. Am I doing ok in my grief journey, or am I going crazy? I need a letter grade or a progress report! I talked with Larry about how I am doing and my feelings that maybe I should be doing better than I am. He reminded me of the standard Hospice bereavement period of thirteen months, and that it exists for a reason. He can be pretty insightful at times! I wonder if sitting in my rocking chair, rocking like crazy with my leg weights on, counts as exercise? Maybe I can invent rocking chair aerobics and make a million dollars! I could bill it as grief therapy and market it to Hospice programs!

Monday, June 12

      "I am crazy, I am crazy. I am nuts. I am nuts. And I'm going bonkers. And I'm going bonkers. Ding Ding Dong! Ding Ding Dong!" (The preceeding is sung to the tune of Frere Jacques as often as necessary!) This little ditty is the result of too little hubby, too much kid time, and not enough good sleep. Grief may also be a part of it as well. I check prices for Mom's grave marker and find out it is cheapest to buy it through the cemetery. It will be a bronze marker in a cement base with Mom's full name, followed by her R.N. initials, date of birth and death, a colonial rose motif and praying hands symbol. It should look nice. I cry after Russ and I make the final choices.

Tuesday, June 13

I almost give myself permission to skip writing tonight. After all, this journal should not be a trap. I have a headache and can't sleep, so I write anyway. Today was Larry's job interview. We are staying at a wonderful bed-and-breakfast that makes it worth the whole process. Even if nothing comes of this job interview, we get a treat! I want to talk to Mom tonight, to tell her how unsettled I feel. I really don't believe God is calling us away from Cheboygan, but if He is, I will willingly go. Especially if this could be a great opportunity for Larry. *Lord, please work in this situation and help us know what is right if Larry is offered the job! I am trusting in You!*

Saturday, June 17

I now skip some writing days. Today is a special family day. They host the dedication of the Lighthouse series postage stamps at the Coast Guard Cutter dock. We attend and then visit the arts and crafts show and the auto show. Larry's aunt and uncle are here and it feels good to have relatives present. Last night they took us out to dinner. It was great not having to cook. Mom would have loved this stamp thing today. Dad would have enjoyed it too. I always figured Dad would die first and I would just have to deal with the complications of ambivalent grief. I had it all planned, that Mom would be around to help me cope when Dad died. It wasn't supposed to happen this way!

Sunday, June 18
  Happy Father's Day. I buy cards for my dad and Larry's dad. Maybe I'll mail them by the Fourth of July! I attend church and then I see a couple of Hospice patients this afternoon. Then we take Larry out to dinner, and Nathan and I visit the beach while Larry and Sam nap. The beach is a big-time solace. I get sunburned, but it is worth it. Tonight Larry and I watch the movie "Forrest Gump." It is good to just relax. This is the first time I feel mellow since Mom died. Maybe I'll sleep well tonight.

Tuesday, June 20
  It is getting easier to skip writing days. It is Michigan summer hot, and I find comfort between my fan and front window. Toni calls today, because God brought me to her mind and she knew she had to call. I am crying, so her call helps. I rock and rock a lot in my kitchen chair. Today's mail brings the cancellation of Mom's Medicaid due to the "death of the only eligible recipient." Yuck! I guess there is no tactful way to say "You died, you're canceled." But still, it hurts.
  Last night's dream was once again in Mom's apartment building. Uncle Bob was there only it wasn't really him, but an impostor. He was after the money he had heard Uncle Bob had won playing the lottery. I should be a fiction writer! Uncle Bob died after an ugly bout with cancer, five months before Mom did. Mom and he were lifelong friends, closer than the in-laws they really were. They looked out for each other, and Mom helped cook for him. Anyway, every Christmas Uncle Bob would give all of us lottery tickets. No one ever won much, but it was fun scraping them off together. Next

Christmas, there will be no Uncle Bob, no lottery tickets, and no Mom. I find another old letter from Mom, with her trademark signature. It helps.

Wednesday, June 21

I work for Hospice tonight. I don't know if it is harder or easier to work with families while I am doing my own grief work. The four hours do pass quickly. The lady is someone's mom. She has chronic lung disease. Her adult daughter is a nurse. She has cute grandsons with dark curly hair, older than my boys. Do I want to care for this woman tomorrow if she is still alive? I don't know. She rested on her left side the whole time. That's the side Mom was laying on when she died. That was always her side to sleep on. Was Mom quietly breathing these same last shallow gasps as this woman? Was Mom dusky and mottled or cold before she died? Marlyss said she was cyanotic. I wish I was there when she died. I'm here for my Hospice patients, but I wasn't there for her. I know I cared for her well before she died, but I missed that final moment. It hurts!

Friday, June 23

I need a break. I need some fun that isn't just grocery shopping! The patient I took care of the other night died early Thursday. I didn't have to go back. Yesterday I took Bonnie to the doctor and the ER after her fall. Tonight her son has an accident and sustains a concussion. I end up in the ER again. *Thank you God that both of them will be all right.*

Saturday, June 24

More than a month later, and I finally unpack. Oh, I've already unpacked my toiletries, but my suitcase with my clothing from that week of Mom's funeral has been sitting out in the garage all this time. Obviously I have too many clothes, or I would have needed those by now! I guess I put it off because I knew somehow it would hurt. I cry as I unpack. I am unpacking from the last trip I will ever take to Mom's. When I see her in heaven I won't need any luggage. It is chilly tonight so I have on Mom's yellow sweatshirt that she gave me just after she got sick. Aunt Ruby and my friend Sherri call tonight. Sherri will be visiting this weekend. *Thank you God for company. It is a welcome distraction.*

Today I miss Mom's voice. I wonder if anyone will ever call me "Sweetie" again. Larry calls me "Hon" and Dad calls me "Sis," but Mom was the only one who called me "Sweetie." She did that often, particularly when I was sad. I can just hear her saying, "Oh, I'm sorry Sweetie." That always made me feel better. Sigh. I seem to be sighing a lot lately.

4. Getting Over This "Gone" Thing

Sunday, June 25

This is a no-comment day. I'm busy being a mom. Nathan is sick and Sammy is teething. Enough said.

Monday, June 26

I have a new old junk-store glider on my porch. Gliding is just as good as rocking. Today I call Toni. We talk about Saturday being the two month marker of her daughter's death and how hard it was for her. On Friday one of her neighbors arrived for the summer and Toni had to tell her about it. It was very tough for her. Toni warned me about the first time that happens to me. *Thank You, God, that in the midst of her terrible pain she can still reach out to me.*

Toni has a hard time saying the actual words, "My daughter died." She tries to avoid it by talking about "funeral week" or "that day," whereas I almost have a need to say the words and tell people that Mom died. It just points out how individual grief is. And of course you can't compare the loss of a child with a loss of a parent. I can't imagine grieving any harder than I am right now, and yet I know that if it was one of my kids, the grief would be even more of a nightmare. While our details of grief are different, talking with Toni is a comfort because we both still are just making it moment by moment.

Tuesday, June 27

I want three days alone in a motel room to sleep, read, and write. Total exhaustion hits today. It is the kind where moving off the couch is a monumental task. I take care of the kids and nothing else. I'm probably catching the bug that they've both had. Or I'm just grieving. Or both.

Wednesday, June 28

How can she just be gone? That same question haunts me over and over. My mind knows that she is in heaven, people tell me she still lives in my heart. But to me, at the moment, she is just gone. I can't call her, write to her, see her, or hear her voice. I have to get over this "gone" thing. I meet with friend in Sault St. Marie today. She is married to a Coast Guard officer, and I met her when they were stationed in Cheboygan. She has boys about my kids' ages. She loves to laugh and is smart and kind. They are moving to Virginia. Today was another goodbye. I cope by shutting down my tears. I don't want to miss her so I've decided I just won't think about it. Now that's real healthy, isn't it?

Friday, June 30

I have underestimated the grief of a five-year-old. Tonight Nathan has a fit of rage. In the middle of it he rips up one of Grandma's funeral programs in front of me. He has been raging before this happens, and at one point Larry tries to talk with him. He just gets madder and madder and finally tears up the program. He asks me if it makes me glad and I tell him no. Later he tries to give away the special things that are keepsakes for him from Grandma. I tell him I'll just hold onto them until he wants them back. Soon after his fit he asks for them back. Then he wants to know if I have any more programs and I give him one. He asks for two, and promises not to destroy them. I give them to him. We talk about tearing up paper as a good way to get rid of grief, but that it's probably better not to tear up special papers. We also talk about punching a pillow.

This reminds me of how Nathan reacted soon after Sam came home with us. He suddenly had a fit of crying and gave away all of his toys to Sam. Eventually, he took them back, but it was a process. This is one intense kid! Oh, Nathan, it breaks my heart to see you hurt like this, and I know Grandma would be sad too. She loved you so much. You were a light in her life. *Oh, Lord help me somehow convey this to Nathan and help Larry and me help him through this.* Tonight I am not sad at the loss of my mom, I am sad at the loss of Nathan's grandma. She was Nathan's very first baby-sitter. I grieve that she won't know Sam, but that is different, because there isn't the history. We all still need you so much, Mom. This is fresh, raw, new pain, because of the pain of my child. How many more times will this feel like a new wound, with rough and ragged edges?

Sunday, July 2

Last night's dream is once again strange and terrible. Mom was alive again, but somewhere in between her embalming and funeral. She walked with a limp, which was damage caused by the embalming. We still knew she was going to die and the funeral was scheduled. My friends are all present. At some point we lose Sammy, but he is returned to us, dropped from an airplane. No wonder I am exhausted when I wake up. I am sad, but I feel close to Mom all day. Although that wasn't the peaceful vision dream that

I've been hoping for, at least I saw her. Today I feel like Mom is just around the corner from my eye. If I turn quickly enough, I'll see her. If I just listen harder, I'll hear her voice. Grief is weird. I do it weird. I hate it. Yuk phooey!

Wednesday, July 5

More and more I am able to skip writing for a day or two. Monday night was hard because Nathan had another rage and took it out on me. Maybe he needs counseling but I don't know who to trust. Yesterday was the Fourth of July. We were invited to an older couple's home, people who have kind of taken us in since we've lived here. They live on a lake and it was wonderful to be fussed over by them. Larry took Nathan to the fireworks and I got to go to bed when Sammy did. This morning the first thing Nathan says to me is "Well, at least we still have one grandma left." I wonder what his brain was processing all night!

Thursday, July 6

Today I get donations from family for Mom's grave marker. We almost have enough for it now. I really need to get that marker on Mom's grave. It makes me mad that money is delaying this. Nathan and I are having a good day today. Last night he found an old postcard from Grandma and he went to sleep holding it. He has also been plugging his ceramic Christmas reindeer in at night. This creation, Rudolph, was Uncle Bob's and Uncle Bob and Mom are linked together in our memories. Nathan has made Rudolph his own, by sticking his Fourth of July flags in his nose and ears. Christmas lights and the old red, white, and blue combined in one creature!

Sunday, July 9
    Reading is comforting right now. I am reading Eugenia Price's third novel in her Georgia Trilogy. The people in it are grieving and somehow it helps. Yesterday was the two-month mark since Mom's death. Time really does pass. It wasn't as hard a time as the first month was. We cleaned and painted some of Nathan's room. Activity does help. Today I feel a burden for my dad. I miss him and I'd like to see him again. I'd like to know where his faith is. I feel that our time remaining is short, somehow. And I miss my brother. Texas and Tennessee seem very far away right now. I will visit Mom's grave in August. Larry and I will go to the farm before my cousin Tom's wedding. We'll spend one night and day before we head to Lansing to the wedding, so there should be time to work a cemetery visit in. I need to see Mom's grave. I still hate saying that word, I hate that Mom has a grave, but I need to see it. Maybe it will give me some peace about that particular issue.

Monday, July 10
    I have a good talk with Jenny today. It is the first time in a while that I've talked specifically about this grief process. I tell Jenny about the mail that is still coming in with Mom's name on it and still having to mail out copies of the death certificate. I also tell her about crying today when I open Mom's lockbox. I was looking for something else, and I stumble across the letter Mom wrote a few years ago. It is a goodbye note to Russ and me. We read it together the week of Mom's funeral, but I haven't looked at it since. Mom really loved us and was so proud of us. We are blessed to have that in writing. I really need to copy it and send it to Russ. It is short and to the point. Basically it covers her wishes for her funeral. It is the last paragraph that gets to me. "Please don't be too sad. Remember all

the good things we shared over the years. You are the greatest kids in the world and I love you very much. All my love, Mom." *Thank You, God, that I still have physical reminders of Mom's love for us.*

Tuesday, July 12

Today I do anger therapy with Nathan. We use a plastic hammer and an old teddy bear of mine. It is exhausting. I am expending a lot of energy helping Nathan deal with his feelings. I am not sure that I am dealing with mine at the moment. Last night I could not sleep even though I was exhausted. I am not dreaming as much, but I am not sleeping deep sleep at night either. I am not sure which is worse: nightmares or lack of sleep. I need to stop right now. I need to say, "Hey wait a minute. Can we just acknowledge one more time what happened? I still need to grieve. I need space." Another sympathy card arrives today. One came last week. *Thank You, God, for keeping these cards coming. I'd love one a week for the next year, if possible, please!*

This journal is beginning to confirm what I've known deep down all along. I am a writer! I've always written, but have been reluctant to describe myself as a writer. This journal is proving it to me. I've been reading Mom's old letters, and when I catch some of the descriptions and detail she included, I can tell that she was a writer as well. Mom, I always knew my love of reading came from you, now it is neat to know the writing does as well! Of course, it is all a gift from the Lord, but I am glad He chose to pass it on to me through you.

I just reread the beginning of this journal. So much happened in just a few pages. On page one Mom is well, then sort of sick, then really sick. A few pages later, she died. How can I ever do justice to all that passed before and after when the pages seem too short and the words too few? Of course, I am using a small notebook, maybe five by seven. Today I buy a full-size bigger notebook. Bigger journal, bigger grief? At least bigger pages to write it on. I had hoped to end this shorter notebook at the three-month stage. Hospice training states that three months is a pivotal point, but I am having a pivotal point at two months. I always was just a little bit contrary! I think two months is hard in its own way. It is a nondescript place, not new and fresh, but not old and familiar either. It is a La-La land of grief. I bet there are other La-La lands waiting as well.

Saturday, July 15

I've been redecorating. Fits of grief inspire fits of activity. Nothing major, just new curtains for the kitchen windows. They are lacy and blue and brighter than what was up there before. I also put up a Victorian style divider to separate my laundry area from the kitchen. I covered the side that faces the kitchen with pink and blue striped fabric and white fringe on the top. Larry even noticed how nice it looks! So now I have a color-coordinated pink and blue kitchen. It is pretty, and right now I need pretty!

Nathan is still having fits of rage. He yells, cries, screams, and kicks at times. Jan calls and prays for us. I cry. Aunt Ruby is coming for a three-day visit tomorrow. All day long I find myself thinking, "When Mom and Aunt Ruby get here..." Aunt Ruby always came with Mom before. She has never been here on her own. In my adult years, I've really enjoyed the combination of Ruby and Naomi, sisters. Whenever we've been together, the three of us would play marathon Scrabble and Trivial Pursuit games. Mom always won Scrabble and Aunt Ruby usually won Trivial Pursuit. Once in a great while I would surprise myself by winning a game. We used to accuse Aunt Ruby of reading all of the answers to the Trivial Pursuit game when she was by herself, just so she would have an edge on the rest of us.

One time when Mom and Aunt Ruby were playing Scrabble by themselves, somehow my aunt managed to get my very gentle mother so riled that she threw down her tile holder and quit the game. I wish I had been there. I rarely saw my mother get mad. I'm not quite sure how I am going to handle having Aunt Ruby here without Mom. I have to remember that she is grieving, too. Her big sister was very important to her. *Dear Lord, help this visit be about enjoying each other and not just about missing Mom. Amen.*

Tuesday, July 18

What a whirlwind. She came, she saw, she conquered. Aunt Ruby's visit was happy and tender and sad and loving. Nathan blossomed and I think I did too. We played Scrabble and baked and ate and cooked and ate and cooked some more. We had Pastor and Mary over for Auntie's birthday dessert party. Her blueberry pie and my flag cake made with strawberries and blueberries were big hits. Aunt Ruby brought real blueberries from South Haven for us. What a treat! It is hard to get the quantities of fresh fruit in Cheboygan that I am used to having access to. We listened to Christian music and sang as loud as we could to the songs we knew. We talked and talked. Aunt Ruby played games with Nathan and sorted socks for me. She had to help with my laundry at least once while she was here. Mom would have wanted it that way! She brought me the painting she had done of the Cheboygan lighthouse. It is a treasure on my wall, along with her other seascape paintings.

Aunt Ruby is the creative sister. She has made everything from homemade ties and Christmas ornaments, to woven baskets and paintings. She now teaches basket-making classes. Other tidbits of fun from our visit: Nathan beating her at cards and laughing hysterically. Taking Aunt Ruby to the beach to photograph scenes for future artwork. Watching Aunt Ruby dicker with a lady over the price of some of her baskets that she is going to sell up here. Aunt Ruby knows how to get the most for her work! Going to Dairy Queen for lunch and McDonald's for breakfast. Sharing stories. She told me that at Mom's funeral dinner she sat down by Nathan and he said, "I was saving that seat for Grandma." Aunt Ruby just hugged him. The last night Aunt Ruby was here she said, "Goodnight Sweetie." It sounded like Mom and I cried. *Someone else will call me Sweetie. Thank You, God.*

Today I have to let Aunt Ruby go. I let Mom go and she never came back. I know this is different, but I still don't like it. I cry when I say goodbye, but I don't experience the gut-wrenching fear that I felt when Mom left here the last time. Maybe that was just a premonition. Whatever it was, I am grateful that I don't feel it when Aunt Ruby leaves. Being with Aunt Ruby has been a relief. I've felt closer to Mom than at any time since she died. Maybe I will make it through this, after all.

Friday, July 21

I make sweet corn and BLTs and cantaloupe for supper. An easy summer supper. I just know that if Mom were here, she'd say, "Oh, that sounds so good!" I have a hard time eating watermelon this summer. She craved that so much this last year. I would buy it and cut it up for her so she could eat it anytime she wanted to. I shut down tears the other day when Aunt Ruby left, because I knew I had to go to work. Big mistake. Now I can't cry. Toni was here delivering Avon and she asked me if I had been able to cry yet. I feel myself pulling away inside, hedging, not letting myself feel.

Numbness is welcome at this point. I think I'll just go with it.

Tuesday, July 25

Suppertime remains the hardest. I want someone to ask about the details. I want someone to care about "what good thing" I am fixing tonight. Mom used to ask me that on the phone. Today the produce truck is in town so we have fresh green beans, sliced tomatoes, sweet corn and muskmelon, cottage cheese and ham sandwiches. All things Mom would have loved. She ate her tomatoes sliced and covered in sugar. Sometimes I eat mine that way. Just like dessert. I still haven't cried since shutting down my tears a week ago. I am on hold. Dried up and shut down. A lovely place to be.

Wednesday, July 26

Today we attend a funeral for someone Larry knew from work. I don't want to go, but I make myself for Larry. I feel my eyes watering during the service, but it is so different from Mom's. The tears don't flow. Today in the mail there is a note from Mildred Smith. I had been thinking about her a lot lately. She is one of the sort of stray people that Mom was famous for adopting. She had been the cook when I was in the hospital at the age of ten. Because I wouldn't eat my breakfast, she made the effort to find out what I liked. From then on I got scrambled eggs and toast instead of oatmeal and hard-boiled eggs! Mildred is a widow, old and lonely. Mom renewed the friendship with her while I was in college, and while she was still able to get out, she came to bunches of our family gatherings. She has had a lot of illness but she always pulls through. She is feisty, even if she is lonely. I never expected her to outlive Mom. I'm sure she didn't expect to either.

It is late at night and hot. Nathan can't settle down and Larry is sprawled in the middle of the bed. I need space. I end up downstairs on the couch. Tears finally come. I am alone with Mom's pillow and white knit scarf. Sobs hurt, but can heal. *Thank You Lord for tears. Is this lostness going to last forever, or will it fade? What will You replace it with? I have to trust at this point that somehow You will fill me again. Is this lostness and grief part of what we carry around with us until we get to Heaven? Is this why we truly are strangers here, not really at home until we are in heaven? Dear God, I am glad you are big enough for my questions. Thank You for your comfort in this moment. Amen.*

Tuesday, August 1

Nathan has Mom's picture in bed with him, hidden under his Big Bear. I leave it alone. Mom, I need to talk to you!

Sunday, August 6

My grief is becoming an old song that I don't want to sing anymore. Other people probably don't want me to sing it anymore, either! I am sure I am boring right about now. We are off of the prayer list at church. It is time, I know. But I still need those prayers. I can't make myself ask to be put back on. I'll just tell people I trust to keep on praying. They probably don't even need to be told. I am trying to make happy times this summer. The beach and playground help. Dear Lord, help me through this week. It is the trip I've been dreading. Down to Larry's parents for a brief overnight, and then to Lansing for my cousin's wedding. He is much closer than just a cousin, as I've always felt more like a sibling to him and his brother. This will be the first Pahl event since Mom's funeral, and my first trip back to Jackson. How am I going to get through it when I can hardly even stand to think about it? The week after is her birthday. August is an action-packed month! I need to visit Mom's grave. I want to visit her, instead.

Wednesday, August 9

I can't cope. I can't pack. I am too tired. There will be time to finish packing in the morning. I retreat to bed.

Wednesday, August 16

I did it. I made the trip. We stayed with Larry's parents and I faced not being able to stay with Mom. I visited the cemetery, and took pictures and answered Nathan's questions about death and the grave. (I'm still waiting for some of those answers myself!) I went alone to the cemetery a second time. I have a secret. I laid down on my back on my mom's grave and took a picture of the clouds and leaves. I know it isn't really her view of the world right now, but somehow in my weird, convoluted brain, it is. We went to the wedding, and had a good time. Tom and Ann Marie will be very happy together. I am glad Ann Marie knew my mom. They acknowledged the absence of Mom and Uncle Bob during their ceremony prayer. It made me cry. The next day, Ruth and Dale took Nathan to spend a few days with them on the farm. All of that extra TLC ought to help. He comes home tomorrow. I've had 4 days of just Sam. I've mainly just rested. I stopped pushing to keep things functioning and I just let down. Tomorrow I snap back to reality.

Monday, August 21

I keep hearing an echo in my brain, a refrain of "Please don't go, Mama." It is the strangest thing, because I always called my mother, "Mom." Nathan and Sam call me mama sometimes, so maybe that is where it comes from. I wake up sometimes with that thought playing in my brain, as if I have been saying it in my dreams. I probably am.

Ruth and Dale brought Nathan home on Thursday and spent the weekend with us. It was a great time for all of us, and the first time that Ruth and Dale have spent any time up here. I think Dale actually got rested. All of these years milking cows twice a day and trying to keep the farm going have really taken a toll on him. Sometimes I am afraid that he'll be the next parent we lose. Anyway, I am delighted that I could open my home to my in-laws, and that we could have such a good time. I even dragged them to the beach, and they aren't really beach people!

Saturday night Ruth and I stayed up late talking. We relived the last two to three weeks of Mom's life. From the trauma of her hospitalization to Ruth calling me to tell me she was dead, we covered it all. Ruth reminded me that she didn't even have to tell me that Mom had died because as soon as she asked me if Larry was there, I knew. I remember saying, "She's gone, isn't she?" and yet thinking that surely I was wrong all in the same instant. That whole time was hard on Ruth as well. She liked my mom and had known her forever. Mom was a nurse and one of Ruth's instructors briefly while Ruth was in nursing school.

Trauma doesn't always mean blood, guts, and gore. There is a type of emotional trauma that takes place when you receive bad news, and it can be devastating. Although not to the same degree, I think Ruth was traumatized by her role in Mom's life and death. It is a unique bond between us, one that not many daughters-in-law share with their mothers-in-law. It is a good bond, in spite of the circumstances. I may just be beginning to turn the corner away from this sense of trauma. At least now I can tell myself that someday this will be easier. I am sad when Ruth and Dale leave, but I can look forward to three or four more batches of company in the next month. *Thank You, Lord, for the presence of people who really know me. It is truly a blessing and a comfort.*

Tonight I am looking at Mom's jewelry. It is bittersweet, but it helps. There are the pieces that are VFW awards, lots of red, white, and blue stuff that she wore with her uniform, and then her bright and cheerful costume jewelry that she wore with her evening gowns for VFW formal events. It's a good thing Mom had VFW, otherwise she never would have had a reason to dress up. Every woman needs an excuse to dress up once in a while! None of this is valuable, but it is now among my treasures.

5. The Wringing of the Cloth

Friday, August 25

    I must be in a funeral state of mind again. Tuesday night we saw Larry's cousins Norwin and Ethel out at the lake cottage that they visit sometimes. Ethel felt badly because she hadn't known about Mom until July. So, I told her the whole story and maybe that stirred things up again. Anyway, I am having bad dreams again. Tuesday night I dreamed that I was trying to talk to Mom's doctor about Mom's condition, and he didn't know either of us. It felt like a slap in the face, and yet it was just a dream.

    Last night, I relived Mom's dying in my sleep. Then I saw Russ and me in her apartment sorting out her things and planning her funeral. The walls seemed lopsided and everything was just slightly out of balance, the way things are in dreams. I wake up missing my family. Then today I get a letter stating a donation was made by the VFW auxiliary to the National Home in Mom's name. It is all done up in a vinyl folder like a diploma, and for a minute I wondered who had graduated from where. This is one more thing that means a lot and I don't know what to do with. It will go in the box with the rest of those kind of things.

    Dad calls today. He sounds old and sad, and he swears a lot.

Dad always swore in normal conversation, maybe I am just noticing it more today. We say we love each other at the end of the call. That is getting easier and easier to say. I am glad we're finding our way back to each other, but we've both missed so much. He really fell off his pedestal for me when I was ten or eleven, and I began to see the alcoholism for what it was, and all of the crud that goes along with it. Then in my teens I realized that the attractions at the bars weren't just the booze, and I lost whatever little respect remained.

When he finally left home and moved to Texas, I was eighteen and in college. I was furious, but relieved. In the years that followed, we shared a few letters, but he didn't come to my wedding. It was just as well, because at that point I am not sure I was ready to be nice. I saw Dad at a couple of family funerals, but it wasn't until I became a mother that I cared about reaching out to him. I called to tell him we had Nathan, and that seemed to open a door for us. Counseling also helped me to forgive, and to understand a little better. I feel like time is running out for my Dad and my brother and me. We'll never again be that little family that lived at Morrell Street, but maybe we can be more than we are today. *Please, Lord, help them find a way past the bitterness and the way back to You. Amen.*

Thursday, August 31

I wake up sad, and cry while I scrub the bathtub. No particular thing, just this same old longing to talk to Mom. End of summer is a peculiar thing. For the first time in years, I can't stand for it to end. I didn't like the change from spring into summer either, but it was because I didn't want time to keep on moving. This is different. I crave the warmth and the sunlight, the waves and the sand at the beach. Northern Michigan winters can be nasty. I pray this one isn't. So today we go to the beach. I am grabbing one more summer day. It is cold and windy and no one else is there. The waves are big and the kids are enthralled by the adventure of it all. The sun has a cool quality to it, different from the hot blazing light I've craved all summer. *Please, Lord, send me a sunlit fall and a white-light winter. I cannot face a winter of darkness.*

Monday, September 4, Labor Day

Like it or not, it is the end of summer. I have just looked back at this journal. Funny, in July I really struggled with the two-month anniversary of Mom's death, and then in August I skip right over the three-month one. My bereavement training taught me that three months would be a milestone. I guess I like my milestones early. I always was just a little bit different.

I just woke up from a nap. This morning we got up early and did the Labor Day Bridge walk, went out for brunch, and came home and slept. I dream deeply during my nap. More dreams of good-byes and letting go. We are all at Mom's, only it is our old house on Morrell street. Mom was dead and we were packing up her stuff because someone else had already moved in. I kept going back into the house to get one more item, to see it one more time. Finally I stood on the steps and rang the doorbell. I knew I needed an excuse to go back in, so I ask if we left Nathan's blanket behind. The lady doesn't invite me in this time, but hands me the blanket and other things and then closes the door. I know now that I can't go back in anymore. The door-closing clicks loudly in my dream. Then we are at the VFW again for the funeral dinner. Laurel is there. We look at photos of Mom. There is one of Mom and Uncle Bob laughing, really laughing hard, and I can almost hear her laugh. I remember thinking that I rarely heard her laugh out loud like that, and I am glad she is so happy. Then there is a photo that makes me cry even though it can't be real because it never happened. In it, she is sick and her mouth is drooping and she can't feed herself. She has chocolate pudding dribbling all down her face. Her hair isn't done and she looks like an old hag. I cry and say, "Oh, that was when she was so sick." But it never happened that way. There was a time some years ago when Mom had Bell's Palsy and her face did droop like that for a time. I wonder if that was what I was seeing in my dream.

 In my dream I felt closer to Mom than I do now. I wish I could hang on to that feeling. Kindergarten starts for Nathan in two days and I just want to talk to Mom. One more missed milestone in our lives. I can't deal with it. I turn on the TV and blob in front of the U.S. Open. Tennis seems safe, unemotional.

Wednesday, September 20

 Nathan started kindergarten a couple weeks ago. I took him on his first day. He looked so grown up and serious. He attends afternoon sessions and rides the bus to school, and I pick him up afterwards. He likes his teacher and the school, and so do I. That is a relief. If ever I need something to go smoothly, it is this transition to real school. Change is hard for me in the best of times, and this isn't the best of times. I skipped writing for awhile.

 I had a terrible time around September 8. Four months seemed awful somehow, a quarter of a year. All that week I cried a lot and felt that primal, wrenching pain again. I thought I was done with that. Today hurts again too. I call my brother, and our conversation is awkward, stilted. He is hurting a lot and I can't do anything about it. I feel even lonelier when we hang up. It is time to get Nathan and I just don't feel right. I feel orphaned when we hang up. I wonder how Russ feels. At least I get to see some of our extended family, he doesn't. There was such a short time when the four of us, Mom, Dad, Russ, and I were a happy family. I want it back and I can't have it.

I pick up Nathan and make it home. I go to the refrigerator to get us a cold drink and getting ice makes me cry. It's just one of those weird things that remind me of Mom. Every time I fill the ice trays I remember how that was always her self-appointed job whenever she visited us. Mom always had to have lots of ice water. She would get exasperated because I would never remember to refill my ice trays. Now I keep my ice trays full. I empty them into bags like she did and run water right back into the trays, just like she did.

What a memorial--full ice trays! Every time I get my own ice water, I remember fixing her glass of ice water when she was in bed for the night, that last week of her life. She would call from the bedroom, reminding me to fill the glass full of ice and then add the water so that it would stay cold longer. Such a simple thing meant so much to her. She always thanked me for doing it just right. I am glad I could do such little things for her. I'd like to do more, right here, right now!

Friday, September 22

Aunt Ruby and her friend Arliss are here. Both Arliss and Aunt Ruby are widows. Arliss really seems to understand grief and she is very sympathetic. I share with both of them about the ice cube trays, and about Mom's mission to keep my laundry done whenever she was here. Arliss agrees with me that it was too soon to lose my Mom, especially when my own children are young. I must be fixated on the point of time when Mom died. Every dream I have lately is about her actual dying. In last night's dream, Mom was in intensive care and Laurel was checking on her for me. Laurel called me to tell me she had died. We were both mad at the nurse for not calling

Laurel sooner. Mom died at 7 a.m. in my dream and Laurel wasn't notified until 9 a.m. The rest of the dream was about me calling everyone to tell them my mom died. I called Pastor and Jan and Jenny after I called the family and I was making travel plans and crying. Then I awoke with that aching longing that lasts all day. The dream was so vivid I felt the raw pain of that first shock of bad news all over again. That phone call from Ruth must be haunting me. I wonder if it ever haunts her as well. Telling me my mother died couldn't have been easy for her.

Tuesday, October 10

Tomorrow is my first birthday without Mom. *Help me, Lord. I don't know how to get through it.* Sunday was October 8, the fifth month since she died. It was a rough day. I found out that Nata's dad died that day. His memorial will be on Saturday. I am sad for her. Last week my friend Jenny took her kids to the Space Center in Jackson. Afterward they visited my mother's grave. That means so much to me. She stood there and talked to my mom. She told me later that now she understands much better about what it means to me to get the grave marker on as soon as possible. She found it disturbing that there is no marker. Jenny has been there for me through all of this, and her understanding goes a long way. I think I am still living in grief time. Time keeps marching on, but I am frozen around Mom's death. It is still the most significant factor in my life.

Tuesday, October 11

Happy Birthday. It is terrible. Dad called ahead of time on Sunday so that he wouldn't forget. I appreciate the thought, but I sure could have used hearing from him today instead. Mom always sent a card, and called me as well. There are no birthday greetings at all in the mailbox this year. Larry's family all sent them, but they aren't here yet. *Thank You, Lord, for friends.* Jenny, Jan, Lynn, and Marilyn all called. Our Pastor's wife visited. Toni called and sent a note, which will probably come tomorrow. Larry and Nathan wish me Happy Birthday and sing to me at supper time. *Thank You, Lord, that this day is almost over.*

Sunday, October 22

It is almost a week now since I've had a terrible time. My birthday was a major turning point. Tonight I take a bath and wash my face. I remember Mom washing her face every night with Noxema. She had a beautiful complexion. I cry and wring my wash cloth until I am exhausted. Maybe I just invented a new therapy. I can call it "The Wringing of the Cloth." That would make a good book title. Anyway, the tub is a safe place to vent. It doesn't harm or scare anyone and I end up feeling much better.

Last night I dreamed Mom was giving birth to a baby. In my dream she had not been sick after all, she was just pregnant, only no one knew. She gave birth to a healthy baby girl, and she was fine. In my dreams I had mixed feelings about having a baby sister, but I was grateful Mom was no longer sick. Now, analysts would have great fun with that dream, wouldn't they? A true clash between life and death, birth and funerals.

Aunt Charlene called today. They had the whole family over so I got to talk to everyone. Grandma has talked to Mom's friend Bea, from the apartment building. Bea has moved to Holt, Michigan, after having a small stroke. So now there are none of the Three Musketeers left at the Otsego. Aunt Charlene and I talk about my brother, and how we aren't in as much contact as we were a few months ago. She reminds me that he has an entire life in Tennessee, and that with Mom gone, the ties here are weakened. I know she is right, and it makes me sad. I miss my family. I am thankful for Larry and the kids, but there is something about that family-of-origin thing that I am grieving now. I miss that connection to my childhood, to people who knew me way back when.

Wednesday, October 25

Hallelujah! Mom's grave marker is in and in the ground. Ruth saw it when she went to the cemetery for other flowers today. She called me. Then I call Jan to share my emotions. We get lost in our own brand of slightly sick humor. From "decorating" a grave to the whole concept of grave blankets, we find stuff to laugh at. It comes down to the fact that decorating a grave is a poor substitute for decorating my life with my mother's presence. I guess it will have to do.

Sunday, November 4

Today I want to call my mom about the news. The headlines and CNN are full of yesterday's assassination of Israeli Prime Minister Itzak Rabin. The older I get, the more I am bothered by tragedies. This is the kind of news that Mom and I would talk about on the telephone. She and my dad both always paid attention to current events. My love of newspapers comes from them. Two days ago we got our first snow. It was hard for me. Snow means winter and winter means holidays and I barely made it through my birthday and I don't have a clue how to cope with Christmas. I make myself start Christmas shopping today, but there isn't much joy in it. This year I will focus on Jesus, church, and home. That is where my joy and strength will be found. I will start new traditions, such as staying home on Christmas Day instead of traveling to Jackson. I really want to buy Mom her annual gift of Estée Lauder perfume or powder. For as long as I've been married, every year I have splurged for her at Christmas and purchased her favorite Estee Lauder. It is a little luxury, one that she would make last the entire year. Last year I also bought her gigantic yellow bath towels. She enjoyed them, but she hardly even got to use them. Now they hang in my bathroom. I like using them. Mom wanted towels big enough to wrap up in, and these are huge. It comforts me every time I wrap myself in them. It is almost a hug from Mom. *Thank You, God, for simple comforts. They help.*

Monday, November 13

    I am mad at those TV people. Tonight on "Chicago Hope" they kill of one of my favorite characters, the hospital lawyer, and I am furious. I can't handle death right now, even on a television show. Of course, that's my fault for watching medical shows.

    Soon I have to get my act together for the holidays. If I am going to get pictures of the kids done in time to send in Christmas cards, I have to get them done this weekend. It feels like that will take a monumental amount of energy.

    The Hospice patient I took care of Thursday night reminded me of my mom. She couldn't talk, but nodded yes or no. As I asked her about pain, I wondered if Mom was in pain when she died. Was she scared, was she suffocating? I can't believe that these questions are still haunting me. Will they always? *Dear Jesus, please keep the rest of my family safe forever, because if it hurts this much to lose my Mom, how could I ever handle losing anyone else? I know grace comes when we need it. I just don't want to need anymore for a very long time!*

Friday, December 1

The holidays are here, and I survived Thanksgiving much better than I thought I would. Of course, Thanksgiving isn't the holiday that I most associate with Mom. As a kid, there wasn't one traditional place to be. We might go to Grandma and Grandpa's or to South Haven to be with Aunt Ruby's family. Sometimes we just stayed home. No matter where we were, Mom always made her traditional cranberry salad. There was always a discrepancy about whether it was really my Aunt Marilyn's recipe or Mom's recipe, but since Aunt Marilyn died while I was still in college, it became Mom's by default! She always put it in a glass dish and topped it with real whipped cream and walnuts in a starburst design. I always thought it looked better than it tasted, because it was a little too tart for me. Everyone else always raved over it though, and more importantly, it was a tradition! Once I met Larry, I always spent Thanksgiving Day with his side of the family, at his aunt's house.

This year was different. I just couldn't face traveling south yet, knowing that I wouldn't be able to see Mom. Instead, we just stayed home. The Wednesday before Thanksgiving was rough. I called Russ. He told me he had visited Michigan in October for work and had seen Mom's gravestone. I wish I had known he was in Michigan. I would have tried to see him. Our phone call was once again slightly awkward. He hassled me a little about not working full-time. I wonder if he resents me mentioning that money is tight. I guess I'll never know. The reality is that I grew up without the stability of a parent at home, as Mom had to work. As long as Larry is able to make ends meet with his job and my part-time work, I will be home with my kids. Too many bad things happened to me because I didn't have supervision, or anyone to turn to. I know my mom always felt terrible about that, and I am determined to be there for my

Love, Hugs, and Kisses

kids as much as possible. I know I can't protect them from everything, but if I can be there after school and during the long summer days, I will be.

Anyway, Russ and I said "Happy Thanksgiving" to each other and hung up. Maybe we'll never be as close as I want us to be, and I guess I am grateful that we have as much as we do. I didn't call Dad and he didn't call me. I kept myself busy by fixing the turkey and pies on Wednesday. One of the reasons I've never enjoyed cooking Thanksgiving dinner is because of the mess it makes. It wasn't so bad when we lived in Leslie, because we had a dining room and I could close the door to the kitchen and we could eat dinner without staring at the mess. In this house our eating area is right in the kitchen, and there is no avoiding someone sitting facing the stove. So I did all of the hard stuff on Wednesday and cleaned up the kitchen that night. I even made Mom's Famous Fudge. It really is a Christmas tradition, her and I sharing the annual fudge-making. Yet I suddenly had a craving for it and decided to make it. I also wanted to find out if I could really do it on my own. I did! I may have also started a new tradition. Fudge at Thanksgiving. Yum!

I found a family at church that didn't have anywhere else to go, and they came over early to spend the day. I reheated the turkey in the crock pot and it turned out moist and tender. I did mashed potatoes and gravy and dressing and spiced beans and dinner rolls, and it was all ready early. It made the house smell wonderful. Having company saved the holiday spirit for me. Now I understand better why Mom, in her darkest days with Dad, cooked big dinners and invited someone over to share it. I remember one dreary Thanksgiving as a teen. Russ wasn't around because he was in trouble again. Dad's drinking out at the bars every night had gotten worse. Mom seemed quiet and withdrawn. Yet between the two of them, they invited a lonely old man who Dad had picked up in a bar. He spent the day with us, smoking his pipe and telling stories. Mom fixed the complete turkey day dinner with all of the trimmings, just for the four of us. At the time, I was just a selfish teen hating my Dad, resenting that we weren't getting together with someone more cheerful. Now, as I look back, I see what a triumph that day was for Mom, and I understand. I, too, have now had my own Thanksgiving triumph!

Today, I am mourning. Another Hospice patient that I cared about died. Between my work as a nurse, and my own family, I am a bit tired of death. I know I haven't had the losses that some have had, but at this point, that really doesn't matter. Pain is pain, and it doesn't help to compare it. I think about some of the patients that have left their mark on me over the years. The three-year-old and the teenager with the brain tumors, the wonderful lady who was dead within a month after her diagnosis of Lou Gehrig's disease, and so many others. Then of course there was my friend Dawn who died the year before we adopted Nathan. She would have been so happy for us when we finally brought home our children. I think now about Grandpa Pahl, Grandma Lockwood, Mom's friend Aunt Betty, Uncle Bill, Uncle Bob, and Mom.

My family is shrinking, and I don't like it. It isn't growing as fast as it is shrinking, and it bothers me that I have all of these memories of people that my children will never know. I suppose every generation feels that way. Older folks who watch all of their friends and family die must wonder who will keep their memories alive. At least I can do that for Mom. I wonder if my dreams are one way of keeping her real. Last night's was very strange, though, and Mom wasn't even in it. I dreamed about the funeral of a priest. His body was all laid out on the floor. Then his entire body caught on fire and his skeleton was propelled by the force of the fire up and out of his skin and into his coffin. That was the signal for the funeral procession to begin. Very strange, and I am not even Catholic. It was graphic and realistic and made perfect sense at the time!

Friday, December 8
     Major stress. Another possible job offer for Larry has been hanging over our heads and now it has become a formal offer. The first job possibility last summer never materialized and I was relieved that we didn't even have to make a choice. Now, Larry has a huge decision to make. *Dear Lord, help us make the right one.* He is succeeding here in Cheboygan, but not really making enough for us to live on. If he takes this new job, he would get a significant pay raise, but I don't think he would be as happy as he is here. *Help us have a sense of peace, Lord, and walk the right path. Please open doors if we should leave and throw up red flags if we shouldn't.* Nathan is acting out a little right now as well. He probably senses the tension as Larry and I try to make the right choice. *Help us to help our son feel safe and secure. Amen.*

Monday, December 18
     Thank You Lord, for a decision. The Co-Op board offered Larry a raise to stay here. We are staying. We are completely at peace with this decision. We put out a fleece and You answered. Thank You, God.

Friday, December 22
     Christmas is only three days away and so far I haven't crashed. In some ways this has been easier than Thanksgiving. I talked to Toni and she said it has been the same for her. At times I

am even more relaxed this year than I've ever been. For the first time since we moved to Cheboygan, we are not traveling to Jackson for Christmas. Without Mom there, I just can't face Christmas Eve and Christmas Day away from home. Some of Larry's sisters are going to visit later in the week, and we'll share gifts with them at that time. I may be overcompensating at some level, though. Or maybe I am just becoming more organized. My Christmas shopping is done, my cards are all done (first time ever this early), the tree and stockings are up. The gifts that need to be mailed are mailed, and the ones that need to be given to friends here are given. Cookies are baked and tonight we went caroling. I did do things slightly different this year. The cookie dough was store-bought refrigerator dough, but the kids didn't care. I also didn't get out all of the decorations this year. I just didn't have the energy for it.

Christmas caroling tonight was special. Just the four of us went, at Nathan's suggestion. We visited six homes and surprised them with songs and candy. We may have started a new tradition.

I also continued a tradition this year. I always buy new pjs and stuffed animals for Christmas Eve for the kids. This year I bought dated Christmas bears again. They were only ten bucks apiece at Kmart, and I think the kids will enjoy cuddling with them. It helps take the edge off of the anticipation just a little to let the boys open a gift on Christmas Eve. I remember my Mom doing something similar for us occasionally, but I think it was just new pajamas without the toy!

A missing piece was filled in for me today. Our old neighbor at the trailer park, Angie, had sent a Christmas card to Mom. I hadn't been able to locate her address to tell her about Mom, so now I could. She included her phone number, so I called her and we had a great talk. She was very sad about Mom, and we shared memories of both of our families in brand new trailers, next to each other. Angie had a new baby at that time, little Michelle, that I just doted on. I was in my early teens, at that age when babies are fascinating. Angie and I talked about Mom's cooking, and she told me she still uses "Naomi's Sugar Cookie Recipe." *One more hole in my heart has been filled. Thank You, Lord.*

    I also received photos of Mom's grave marker today. My sister-in-law Nancy took them for me. It helps to see it. It also seems strange that so many others have seen it in person, and I haven't.

    Another desire was filled this week. Sometime in the last two months my diamond slipped out of my engagement ring. I was devastated but we couldn't afford to replace it. Larry's Christmas bonus took care of that, and tonight I have a diamond back in my engagement ring, and it is back on my finger. *Thank You God, for not only taking care of my needs, but also my desires. It is a perfect Christmas gift. Now as I focus on celebrating the birth of my Savior, help me to teach my boys the true meaning of Christmas. Help them learn to love and trust in You. Amen.*

Monday, December 25

    Merry Christmas, Mom! I wonder what Christmas is like in heaven? Do you celebrate Jesus leaving heaven and coming to earth for our sakes, or is heaven so much a constant celebration that you don't need to? I wonder. Today is going well. Quiet and peaceful here at home, after the mad rush this morning as little boys tore into wrapping paper. This afternoon I am putting photos in albums. It helps to see family pictures, pictures with Mom and Uncle Bob. This is the first Christmas without them both, although Uncle Bob was in the hospital last Christmas. Christmas Eve yesterday was teary for me, but special. Nancy sent pictures of Sam's adoption, and of course

I remembered Mom being in the hospital at that time. *Mostly today I feel a sense of Your presence and Your peace Lord, and I am thankful.*

6. This Is Grief

Monday, January 1

    I am sick. A sinus infection is making me tired and run down. I miss Mom, Uncle Bob, and the rest of my family. Last New Year's Eve, Uncle Bob died. A year ago today, we were getting ready to go to his funeral. At that point I didn't have a sense that Mom only had a few months to live. She seemed to be doing so well. I wonder if there were warning signs that I missed. That last morning when I saw Mom alive, I obviously sensed something then. Otherwise I wouldn't have fought with myself about going back upstairs to say one more goodbye. I was afraid to leave, afraid I'd never see her again. I wish I would have listened, and gone back for that last goodbye. If I have learned nothing else from Mom's death, it is this: I listen to my instincts. If my gut says to call someone, I don't put it off. If I feel like it is important to write to someone, I do it. If I feel I need to say "I love you" or "you matter to me" I do it. I suppose you never get rid of all of the "if onlys" in the world, but I am doing my best to get rid of all mine!

    When I tell people about this, they tell me that I should have no regrets. I did everything and more for my Mother. In a way that is true. The last year of her life we talked, I was with her, I took care of her as much as I could. And in the five years before that, we had grown as close as any adult daughter and mother could be. Yet, I do have regrets. I wish I had asked her more questions about the past. I wish I had told her more about myself. I wish I had gone to counseling sooner, and dealt with the past sooner. My mother was always silent about my Dad's drinking during their marriage. In the early years of my marriage, I couldn't understand that. She was clingy towards me at that time, just as she was when I first went away to college. I didn't understand then how much my success mattered to her. I only knew I had to break away, and I did. I came home to her during those college years for weekends and vacations, but I was fighting for my independence every step of the way. Fortunately, she loved Larry, so that made it easier for me to stay away with him for long hours. I didn't really understand then how lonely she was. Dad had left, and Russ and Gwen moved to Tennessee. Russ had straightened out his life by then, they had two boys and Russ was doing well in his job. Mom was happy for them, but missed them terribly. Once I was married, even though we only lived a short distance apart, I limited my visits and phone calls. We helped her out financially, and once I even hired her to help me with housework when I was working full-time.

In those early years of my adulthood, I only saw her as a victim of my father's alcoholism. I didn't understand then that she was a survivor. Oh, I knew that everything good that we had as kids came from her. I know that she pinched pennies to make sure we had good things to eat, and that the fun times were because of her arrangements. Yet at that point I didn't recognize her strength. It took an incredible determination to work full time at the doctor's office, raise a family, participate in VFW, and try to keep her kids safe and cared for in an alcoholic home. She did the best she could,

Love, Hugs, and Kisses 97

but I wasn't ready to recognize that then. As I got older, and that milestone year of thirty began to appear, I became more appreciative of Mom. Yet I was still a little resentful of having to help her financially. I told myself that I blamed Dad, and yet there was a part of me that didn't understand why Mom didn't have more money. Now I see that she took lower paying jobs for the trade off she received in flexibility and free health care from the doctors she worked for. Unfortunately, that limited her retirement and her job skills, so at the age of sixty when she tried to return to hospital work, which would have paid better, it was too hard for her. She did work at a nursing home for a while, and was loved by the patients, but eventually that got too much for her. Her health was beginning to suffer already at that stage, but no one really recognized it.

    When Mom chose early retirement at age 62, I supported it. By that time, Larry and I had come to terms with helping her financially and we were both ok with it. I was thirty, working at a great part-time job at the health department, we had left the family farm and Larry was working in Leslie at the Co-Op. We weren't building up any savings, but we were cleaning up our share of the debt from the farm and we were doing better. We had found a place for Mom to live with a friend of hers, after the trailer almost fell apart around her head. It wasn't ideal, but with our help, she was making it.

    Then little Mister Nathan Allan Crouch suddenly arrived, and everything changed. Mom became a doting grandmother and I loved sharing my new happiness with her. Everyone was thrilled for us. It had been years since there was a new baby on either side of the family, and he charmed the socks off everyone. I took a three-month leave of absence, but soon knew I couldn't go back even to my part-time job. I had waited too long to be a parent. I couldn't leave my baby so soon. However, without my income, we were in a bind. We also couldn't help Mom out, and she was hurting. I could take an on-call every-other-week position at the Health Department, and make enough to tide us over. The only problem was, we still wouldn't be able to help Mom and I wouldn't have anyone to leave Nathan with if I got called out before Larry got home from work.

It was my husband who came up with the brilliant idea of moving Mom in with us. We had room to put in a bathroom and another bedroom in the basement, and although I was scared, I agreed that it seemed like a good solution. Mom was delighted, because her living situation had begun to deteriorate. It never occurred to me that it wouldn't work, because we had always enjoyed each other's company and we seemed to be closer than ever. The only one that had any reservations was my mother-in-law, who said that she loved her mother dearly but couldn't live under the same roof. I listened, but didn't give those reservations much credence.

In August, only three months after I had become a new Mom, my mom moved in with us. Her bathroom wasn't done, but Larry had walled in a bedroom and although it wasn't finished, it was adequate to start out with. The first couple of weeks were fine. I fell into some bad habits, though. As a new mom, I was constantly tired. I got into the habit of sleeping in and letting her get up with Nathan. Then when I got up, I would often find that she had done my housework for me, and that there wasn't much else to do other than cook. We still did enjoy cooking together, and of course, Nathan was just our little sunshine.

Soon, though, I began to feel the stress of a turf battle. I was insecure as a new mom, and worried that Nathan would get mixed up on who was his mom and who was his grandma. I also felt the stress of not having any time alone. Even though Mom took an afternoon nap and always went to her room after supper, I began to feel closed in. Once, when she visited Aunt Ruby for a few days, the relief was huge. I felt guilty all the time, and began to quibble with her over little things. Larry noticed the change in my attitude and how critical I was becoming. I also was becoming angrier by the day.

I had never known that I carried any anger whatsoever against Mom for my childhood. I had always seen her as my stability growing up. I didn't realize that I harbored bad feelings toward her for leaving me unprotected after fourth grade when my parents decided I didn't need my full time baby-sitter anymore. I was left alone in the summers and after school, and I was a sitting duck for the abusive situations I fell into. Now I wonder if I would have been safer with an adult around. Certainly, it would have made it easier for me to say no. Hopefully, an adult would have been curious about my prolonged absences from home, and might have even asked a few questions.

Anyway, I always thought I blamed Dad for all of that. With my mom living with us, I would find myself snapping at her and criticizing her for no reason. I became physically ill, and depressed. It all came to a head one day at the end of November when we were in Nathan's room together. I had him on the changing table, putting on a new diaper, and Mom and I were talking about some minor repair that needed to be made in the house. I told her Larry would get to it when he could, but it would probably take some time. She made an innocent comment that Larry was just like my dad when it came to getting home repairs done, meaning that it took a lot of time.

I exploded. I yelled at her for daring to compare my sober, faithful, wonderful husband to my drunken cheat of a father and I burst into tears. Poor Nathan. He lay on his changing table, and I put my head down on his little tummy and cried my eyes out. He never let out a peep, and I felt his little hands holding onto my hair. Mom apologized, and went downstairs. I felt awful, and asked her to stay with Nathan. I drove into town and to a friend's house. I poured out my story, and she convinced me to go for counseling. I knew we couldn't afford to pay much, so I was able to find a Christian counselor at our church. I had been in counseling once before, to learn how to communicate better with my husband. However, that had been short-term, and we had never, ever dealt with my past.

Now, it was time. In that first session, Shirley, my incredible counselor, convinced me to make different living arrangements for Mom, no matter what it took. I had everyone at church praying about it, and God made a miracle happen. When I called the senior housing commission, it turned out that because Mom was living in an unfinished basement, that classified her as homeless. She shot up to a number one priority on the waiting list, and within a few weeks they had an apartment for her at the old Otsego Hotel. She couldn't move in until the first of February, but just knowing it was going to happen took the pressure off both of us.

Plus, I was in weekly counseling by then, and for the first time ever, I was coming to terms with my painful past. I saw my parents for who they really were, both the good and the bad, and I began to forgive. It freed me up to relate to Mom in ways I never had before, and we became equals and even closer friends. Mom moved to her new home in February, and thus began an incredibly happy time for us. I took a new job at Visiting Nurses in Lansing, working just one day a week. Mom came to our house to baby-sit and even after paying her, I was making as much as I had in the on-call position.

The only fly in the ointment was Larry's job. His company was bought out by another, but they kept him on, working in sales out of St. Johns. It had increased his driving time by an hour every day,

Love, Hugs, and Kisses **101**

plus sales weren't really his thing. We knew we either had to move closer to his work or he had to find another job. We put the house on the market but absolutely nothing opened up. God had a plan, but it didn't involve us staying anywhere close by.

In January of the following year we heard of a job opening for manager of Cheboygan Co-Op. We had never even heard of Cheboygan, but once we saw on the map how close it was to Lake Huron, I was willing to move. By then I was finishing my counseling, and I felt stronger emotionally and spiritually than I ever had. Physically, I had been sick for months with a severe respiratory infection, and we were hoping that a move to a new environment would help.

As much as I loved our little house in Leslie, it was damp, and the doctors had begun to suspect that mold was the culprit that was destroying my respiratory system. Even though we would be four-and-a-half hours away from family, when Larry got offered the job, we knew it was the right decision. We both felt a peace about it and a certainty of God's leadership. God had provided a buyer for our house, and allowed us to find a new home in Cheboygan in our price range, on a land contract and ready for immediate occupancy. So in February, a year after Mom had moved into her new apartment, we packed up the car and the truck and the moving van and away we went. Mom and a friend went with us to help me settle in, and they stayed a couple days. When they left I was sad, but excited about our new adventure. I would stay close to Mom with phone calls, visits and letters, and I just trusted it would be ok. I never imagined I would only have Mom for three more years.

Tuesday, January 7

I just reread my writing from above. What a blast from the

past. I am dealing with having no regrets. Although our time was short once we moved to Cheboygan, during that time my friendship with Mom blossomed. She was so happy about both of her children. It meant the world to her that Russ and I both had happy marriages and our own houses, something she never had. She was proud of us, and she and I rejoiced in the bond we shared in Christ. During those last years, we talked more about faith than we ever did, and I got an even better appreciation of the fact that Mom truly was a strong woman. So I guess I really can't have too many regrets, just longings. Longings for more heart-to-heart talks, more letters, more hugs. This then, is grief. No matter how much time you have with the one you love, it isn't enough. Maybe this longing is from God, to help us begin to understand the longing he has for us.

7. Gifts That Come

Friday, February 2

Probable miscarriage. After all these years of infertility. I want Mom. The doctor shrugged me off and my gynecologist is out of town. I call my mother-in-law. Ruth listens to my story, and as a nurse and a mother of eleven, confirms what I know in my heart. Larry looks at what I passed and agrees it is a miscarriage. After days of horrendous bleeding, the flow stops almost immediately after that last bout of cramping and the passing of that little something. I take a picture of that little bit of white tissue, and I grieve. *Dear God, help me. A soul that I didn't even know has left my body and I am bereft.*

February 20

I haven't written and I haven't written. The days after my miscarriage were awful. It happened on a Friday night, after days of heavy, awful flowing. I had messed up on my pill and stopped taking it for a while. I guess in my grief I just stopped thinking about what could happen if I didn't take that little pill every day. I had been on it for years strictly to control my cycle. Yet somehow this winter I just didn't worry about that anymore. Who knows, maybe I even hoped for a miracle of healing and pregnancy. Anyway, one day I started flowing and it just got worse and worse. My cramps intensified on Friday, and Friday night in the shower I passed this clump of white tissue. My cramps ceased soon afterwards, and my bleeding slowed down. I called the medical doctor on call because my gynecologist was out of town. He didn't pay much attention because of my history of infertility, and told me that I probably just passed a blood clot. A blood clot would not have been that color. I should have just gone to the ER. Then I might have had closure. Instead I was left in doubt.

By the time my gynecologist got back he was booked solid but ordered a blood test. That was negative, but he said the test was far enough away from the event that it wouldn't have been conclusive. So, I was left with more doubt. I was still having some physical pain and not feeling well, but I tried to just get on with things. God put me in touch with a couple women who had been through it, and they were supportive and helpful. I finally got in to see my gynecologist today. It was my annual appointment, but I should have asked for an appointment sooner. I am really sick--fever, chills, etc. I have a massive pelvic infection with endocervitis. The doctor confirms that I probably did have a miscarriage. Antibiotics will heal my body, but what will heal my heart? I need to talk to Mom.

Friday, March 1

Today I prepare our car to be sold. We bought Aunt Charlene's used minivan at a great price. Now it is official. I am a minivan Mama! Anyway, we need to sell our little red colt. A buyer is coming tonight. I take it to the car wash and the gas station. I don't expect grief, but I get grief anyway. This is the car we brought both of our babies home in. I picture Mom sitting in the seat beside me, as she did so many times. I almost feel her presence physically. When the car is gone, so is one more place of her physical presence. One more place where she was.

    We sell the car tonight and I try to relax and vegetate. I watch a beautiful television show, a tribute to the pairs ice skater Sergei Grinkov, who died suddenly on the ice of a heart attack in November. The show was put on by his wife and partner, Ekatereena Gordeeva and his friends and peers. Katia and Sergei truly were magic on the ice. As she skates alone tonight, with her arms outstretched in some of her signature moves, without him, you can almost sense him by her side. I cry. What doesn't make me cry these days? She has a little girl to raise all alone. *Oh, Lord, please help and comfort them.*

    I don't really talk about my miscarriage, but it haunts me. Last night I dreamed about giving birth to a baby girl. It was very real and powerful, and even though I've never given birth I could feel the labor pains in my sleep. A few nights ago I dreamed that I left Nathan and Sam at Ruth and Dale's to go to a funeral. I heard my voice saying, "I'm sick and tired of leaving you two to go to a funeral." I must still be in a funeral state of mind.

Tuesday, March 19

    Since my miscarriage, I miss Mom more than ever. I dream every night about places we shared. Last night we were at my grandmother's old house and I was sleeping there again like I did as a little girl. I dream a lot about Mom's apartment, our old house on Morrell Street, Laurel's apartment, South Haven. I almost never dream about the trailer. Once in a while I dream about Larry's and my house on the farm or in Leslie. Always a very tangible place. When Mom died, I lost not only a person but my sense of place. No more home base to return to, at least not on my side of the family. The closest family home we ever really did have was that rented house on Morrell street. That is the one I dream of most. Both of my grandparents' houses are sold now, and Aunt Charlene and Aunt Pat are in a new house, one they bought this winter. At least Aunt Ruby is still in the same place and so am I. I am thankful Mom visited this house, and I have memories of her in my kitchen and living room.

    I am aware of my blessings. I do smile and laugh more often now. Aunt Charlene and Aunt Pat have been wonderful and care deeply. Aunt Ruby loves me as well. Larry's family and parents have been phenomenal and shower my kids with love. Dad calls once in a while and so does Russ. I have Larry, Nathan, and Sam, my greatest blessings. My worst nightmares center around losing one of them. A couple of weeks ago I dreamed the boys were kidnapped and we never got them back and the whole dream was two years of desolation until I woke up. It seems that all of my dreams are still about searching for something. *Dear Lord, please help my dreams change to finding something!*

Saturday, March 30

    As anniversary time approaches, my fear of losing someone else is worsening. I've always had a little paranoia in this area, but now it is definitely worse. I think about Uncle Bob dying one year, and Mom dying a few months later, and I wonder who will be next. Tomorrow Larry and Nathan and a group from church are driving two hours away to see a passion play. Sam and I aren't going because it is just too big a trip for him. I am almost afraid to let my other two guys go. I am afraid they will get in an accident. Last week Larry and Nathan went to the karate tournament and I was sad and nervous the entire day. I worry about an accident or something happening to Nathan at school or about Sammy's asthma worsening. *Lord, I know you don't want us to live in fear. In the name of Jesus and by the power of His blood, please remove this bondage of fear and surround me with your strength and peace. In the name of Jesus please cast out this fear and grant me your joy. Amen.*

Friday, April 5, Good Friday
Church was very worshipful today, Lord. Nathan asked lots of questions about all of this "Jesus stuff." Thank you for giving me words. Please help him find his way to you, Oh Lord.

Sunday, April 7, Easter Sunday
My favorite holiday of the year. *Thank you God for a day of rejoicing!* We had a worshipful service, and I invited company for dinner. Everyone enjoyed my ham made "Mom" style with her traditional Vernors, pineapple, and brown sugar glaze. We laughed and joked and I felt genuinely happy. *Thank You, Lord.*

Monday April 22
Mom got sick for the last time one year ago today. Yuck!

Wednesday, April 24
Toni's daughter died one year ago today. *Help her in her pain, Lord.* At karate today, a friend was sharing about her father's new diagnosis of congestive heart failure. It was scary listening to it. I worried that he might go through the same thing Mom did. Ruth called last night. We had donated flowers to the church in Mom's memory, and my sister-in-law Nancy took them out to the cemetery and put some on Mom's and Uncle Bob's grave. Ruth said it got her stirred up and she went back and reread her own journal from last year at this time. She relived all of Mom's illness, especially that day when Mom suddenly turned bad while Ruth was visiting her. That

made an incredible bond between Ruth and I, and I will always be grateful that Ruth was with her.

    I think these next two weeks will be the hardest. I have an ominous, superstitious fear of someone else dying between now and May 8. *Dear Lord, I know this feeling isn't of you and I give it over to you to control. I pray Ephesians 6 and ask you to keep my family safe. Help Dad and Russ come to know you. I miss Dad right now. I sort of want to see him and yet I wonder if I would still be afraid to be real with him. I miss Russ. He is going his own way in Tennessee and I am doing the same thing here. Oh, Lord, I miss all of my family right now. Please keep Aunt Charlene and Aunt Pat and Aunt Ruby and Russ and Dad and Larry's family all safe. Please help me through the next two weeks.* My anxiety escalated starting with the anniversary of the Oklahoma bombing. That was the last time I talked normally with Mom. I called her just to hear her voice because it seemed like the world was going crazy and I just wanted to talk to my Mom. That was the last time she was Mother and I was Daughter. From then on, I took care of her. Mommy....

Saturday, May 4

    A year rapidly approaches. I call Russ today to say Happy Birthday. I've already talked to him twice this month and it is only four days into it! He can't believe it has been a year since Mom died. It has dragged for me and gone fast at the same time.

Wednesday, May 8

    Happy Anniversary! Mom, how can you have been gone a year from my life? Today I get out my journal and relive everything I was doing a year ago. It still seems fresh somehow. I can remember everything I felt that day, but I can't remember the sound of your voice. Today I can't concentrate on anything. I am supposed to have an agenda done for youth group tonight and there are other details I know I need to attend to and I can't. I feel like I should be turning a corner now that it has been a year and I'm not sure that I am. Both Laurel and Rita tell me that it isn't easier once a year has passed, just different. I think that they are right. *Lord, if I need to turn a corner pretty soon you're going to have to guide me because I don't think I can find my way around it by myself!*

Thursday, June 13

I am doing better. Joy strikes in my children's laughter, at the beach in the way the sun sparkles on the waves. It is still too cold for swimming, but the majesty of the lake soothes me. Grief has taught me to function in a new landscape. There are familiar people who are mountains in my landscape. Larry, my family and friends, stand tall and strong for me. The mountain of my relationship with Mom is missing, and in its place is a crater. The security of being a daughter, of having Mom to lean on is gone, and in its absence is a hole that I suspect will never fill. But I am learning to be ok with that. More often now, I can negotiate my way around the crater. Sometimes my memories build a bridge over the crater and that is wonderful. Sometimes the bridge fails. Sometimes I fall into the crater and wallow in the deepest pit of it. This is still grief. I no longer fear it, though. I know now that there is always a way out of that crater. *Dear God, thank you for lifting me out of the crater when I fall. Thank you for helping me to build bridges over the crater. You truly do "lift me out of the slimy pit, out of the mud and mire." You truly do "set my feet on a rock and give me a firm place to stand." Psalm 40:2*

Tuesday, June 25

Something wonderful has happened, Mom. Your daughter is finding her wings. I prayed about it, and I did it. I went to the newspaper with some sample columns, and I am now a columnist for the *Cheboygan Tribune*. My column will appear weekly on the religion page. I guess I'll find out now whether or not I really am a writer. I wouldn't have done this a year ago, or two or three years ago. I am stronger now, more independent. I can take this risk now. I will always be your daughter, but I am becoming my own woman now in a brand new way. I know you would be proud of my writing, and you would praise it even when you didn't understand it. I would write wondering what you would be thinking, and worrying that you may be hurt when I mention our family history.

So, there is a trade-off. I no longer have my mother here on earth, but I have freedom to be myself and to write openly and honestly. It isn't a fair trade. I would rather have you. But since I can't, I would be a fool to ignore the gifts that come from grief. Writing has always been a gift, and this new freedom is a gift bought with a heavy price. I pray that God will bless this gift and help me to use it wisely. And even though they probably don't have newspapers in heaven, Mom, if you get a chance, read my column once in a while!

Saturday, July 27

Grief still hits, but the need to write about it is lessening. Maybe because I am writing weekly for the paper, the need to do other writing isn't as strong. This week my fifth article appeared. People seem to be responding well. I keep praying for ideas.

Tears are building this week. I want to talk to Mom. There was a horrendous plane crash a couple of weeks ago and no one knows for sure if it was a bomb. Then there was a bomb today at the Olympics, killing one person and injuring 18. It reminded me of last year, just before Mom got sick, when the Oklahoma bombing occurred. I called Mom, feeling sick about it, and we commiserated together. That was just the kind of thing we did. Today I want to call her and hear her say, "Isn't it a shame?" and "What is this world coming too, anyway?" I want to send her my columns and hear her tell me that she "thoroughly enjoyed" reading them. Mom never just enjoyed something, it was always "thoroughly" enjoyed!

Thursday, August 8

The Olympics are over. My new buddy, Nicole, went back to Kansas this week. She worked at our church all summer and we got close. I will really miss her. Letdowns like this still affect me deeply, deeper than they used to. They always make me miss Mom. Tonight I am wearing Mom's pearl ring. I need it.

Tuesday, September 3

Grief is chronic, with remissions and exacerbations, just like a chronic illness. This latest remission has been a long one, and I thought I was over the worst. Then another milestone hits and I crash. Today Nathan started first grade. I cry because he is growing up and because he is in school all day, and Mom isn't here to talk to about it. I cry because Sammy misses his brother and cries and says "no Nay-Nay" when we leave Nathan at school. I never got to share these first days of school with Mom, and I never will. It hurts and it makes me mad!

This exacerbation has been smoldering a while, starting with a new nightmare last week. This was a violent dream, in which Mom was being shot to death by the mob. I saw them coming and I saw her die in my dream, a horrible, bloody gruesome death. This dream haunted me for two days. I told Jenny about it. She pointed out that she has wondered if my feelings about not being there when Mom actually died are still an obstacle for me. After all, Mom died less than twenty four hours after I left her. If I had known her time was that close I would have stayed. I am a Hospice nurse. I am present at the deathbed. But I wasn't present at Mom's. Jenny's words were like an arrow that landed true in my conscience with a zing. I have to deal with this. Since I talked to Jenny I've had one more dream. In it I was trying to reach my mom by phone and I kept repeating her phone number out loud. Her phone number is a recurrent theme in both my dreams and my conscious thoughts of her. I called her so often these last few years and I miss it terribly.

I feel a constant pressure and a dread to deal with this last issue. I have cried all day today. When Nathan went to school, when Sammy complained about missing him, when a silly kid's show let a cricket die in a lame attempt to teach their young viewers about death, I cried. Tonight when Nathan was snippy with me about bedtime, I cried. After the kids are in bed I watch a sentimental rerun on t.v. and I cry.

I am fearful now. Larry is working late and I can't sleep and I am obsessing about what I would do if anything happened to him. Now that I know how much it hurt to lose Mom, I can't bear the thought of losing anyone else. *Dear God, I know this fear isn't of you. I know you are with me in my grief and that you have helped me all along. Please help me trust you and trust you to take care of my guys when I am not with them. Amen.*

I miss the chance to make more good memories with my Mom. She was so enjoying life in those last few years, with her burdens eased and with knowing her kids were happy and raising their own families. I wanted more of that time. I just wasn't ready to let Mom go and I really wasn't expecting her death quite so soon. I truly believed I would have that deathbed scene with her that I've had with so many patients.

Not knowing how she died and what it was like for her is harder because of my Hospice experiences. I want to know if she followed the normal stages or if she just suddenly quit breathing. Was she afraid? Did she know she was dying? Was she gasping for air? Did she try and call out? Or was she comatose? Did she pray? Did she sense Jesus waiting for her? *Oh, Dear Lord, I know that there aren't answers and her death would hurt me anyway but this is such a missing piece for me. Is there any way to fill it in?*

I did not want Mom to die alone. Aunt Charlene says that we all die alone anyway. I know that in one sense that is true, but I also know what it means to family to be there. I know patients who have become more peaceful when family arrived as they were dying. I know Mom's friend Camilla was in the next room, so Mom's death couldn't have been loud or she would have heard. I wonder if Mom had a death rattle. Some people do and some don't. I think Camilla would have heard a rattle. After all, Mom's apartment wasn't very big.

There are two scenarios that may have happened if I had been there the night Mom died. If I had been aware that she was dying, I can't be sure what I would have done. I might have felt obligated to call an ambulance because we didn't have a do-not-resuscitate order and I'm not sure what my brother would have wanted at that point. I might have been too afraid to just let Mom slip away. The old nursing habits from before I became a Hospice nurse could have kicked in. I may have called 911 instead of just holding Mom's hand. I know another trip to the hospital and another bout on the respirator is not what she wanted.

    The second scenario would have been even worse for me. If I had been spending that night with Mom, and if I had been unaware that she was dying, I would have been asleep in the next room on the couch. I would have totally freaked out if I had been the one to find her that morning, knowing that I was present, yet missed her death anyway. That would have been worse than not being there at all. The night of her death Mom had a fall in the bathroom, and Camilla had to call the paramedics for help because she couldn't get Mom back up. Because Mom was conscious and coherent I probably could have gotten her cleaned up and back to bed on my own. I would have sat beside her bed for a time, and once she was asleep I would have gone into the living room. Fatigue would eventually set in and I might have dozed and awakened just before the nurse was due at six a.m. Checking on her and finding her dead would be devastating. I would have blamed myself for not knowing what was happening to her. If that had happened, my nightmares now would be even more terrible.

    Now that I have written these scenarios out I can see that God was merciful in not allowing me to be there. I think Mom did die peacefully. Her heart probably just slowed down and stopped. Her breathing would have slowed, becoming more and more irregular with long periods of apnea (no breaths). It would have been dark and quiet and she probably wasn't in any pain. I don't think she would have resisted death. Mom had already said her good-byes on the phone to Russ and I, although we didn't realize it at the time. She told us she loved us and thanked us for everything. She was at peace with her kids and at peace with her Lord. Although on some level she may not have been ready to die (she had told me she had lots to do yet), she was probably as ready as most people are. Her last illness had drained her and she was terrified of becoming an invalid. If she was at all aware that she was indeed dying that night she probably was accepting. Her biggest fear would be that I would grieve too hard. She would have wanted me to come to terms with her death, to accept it and to rejoice again. Can I do that now? Can I accept her absence in my life? Only time will tell.

Friday, October 11

A second birthday without Mom. I am truly able to celebrate this one. My last journal entry did help me clear a hurdle. I have had no more nightmares about Mom's death since writing out that death scenario in my last entry. I think I finally believe that Mom probably died peacefully. I am accepting that she did it without me, and she did it well, on her own terms, at home in her own bed. It is a blessing and a mercy to die that way, and I am grateful. *Dear God, thank you for never, ever leaving me during this journey. Thank you for being my solid rock. Thank you for the family and friends that have, and still are, helping me through. This journey isn't over, but I am traveling in a better place these days. Thank you that my path doesn't keep me trapped in the "valley of the shadow of death," but travels from low places to high places and in-between places and back again. Thank you that it is all progress and that the high places now outnumber the low places! Amen.*

8. The New Beginning

Grief doesn't necessarily end, but it does change. As my grief became less of a solid block of pain and more of an intangible and haunting breeze, so did my journaling methods change. Instead of keeping a handwritten scrawled account in my old spiral notebook, I now write the occasional newspaper column about Mom. I still get choked up at times, and there are moments when I break down and cry just because I miss my mother. However, with each passing day the memories of the joy we shared grows stronger. I translate that joy into my columns, and in some small way, Mom is with me again.

I decided to share just a sample of my "Mom" columns at the end of this book. They first appeared in *the Cheboygan Daily Tribune*, and have been amended slightly since then. They are very different from my grief journal, but that is okay, because my grief is different now. I also share a resource page. Grief is normal, but it can turn into complicated grief. There may come a time when help is needed to get through it. If someone reading this is in doubt as to whether or not they need help, I encourage them to contact one of these resources.

9. Columns for Mom

Mom's Famous Fudge

One of my favorite holiday traditions from childhood was the making of cookies and candies with my mother. Even my older brother got into the act. I can remember fighting with him over the chance to scrape the fudge pan, and usually losing. I also recall divinity and pecan pralines falling onto wax paper sheets on our dining room table. I was too young to appreciate wonderful creations like pecans so Mom would always make one or two "just pralines" for me. I don't carry on all of her traditions, but I have adopted the making of the fudge as my own. Now I make the fudge at Thanksgiving and Easter as well as at Christmas, but basically I still follow her recipe. Here then, is Mom's Famous Fudge (with my own editorial comments!):

(1) Assemble utensils. This includes the heaviest, hardest-to-wash 3-quart saucepan in your kitchen. Have on hand at least two long-handled wooden spoons because it is a given that one will disappear. One slightly faded two-cup Tupperware measuring cup is a necessity because no other measuring cup will measure the same. Measuring spoons are optional.

(2) Assemble ingredients. We just left them in the grocery

bags until we needed them, but one can be organized and set them out on a table. Ingredients: Sugar and lots of it because we always ran out and had to borrow some, salt, miniature marshmallows (because the big ones don't stir right), butter or margarine (in sticks--it will matter later), small cans of evaporated milk because they fit the recipe exactly and we were always too lazy to measure from the big cans, a variety of flavored baking chips (chocolate and peanut butter are our favorites but in the last few years I got daring and messed around with vanilla and butterscotch), and vanilla extract.

Nuts are optional, but if you include them, add to the utensil list an old-fashioned nut grinder that screws on top of a jar and gives one something to gripe about. Or nuts can be ground with my new improved method of placing them in plastic bags on the floor and having everyone jump on them until all their aggression is relieved (heavy boots help this process)! Nuts must be the hard-to-find and more expensive black walnuts because plain walnuts just don't smell as enticing when stirred into the fudge.

(3) Begin fudge. Pour 2 1/4 cups sugar into pan. If you obeyed instructions and are using the right measuring cup it just means filling it to the brim one time and then dumping it into the pan when it is about to overflow.

(4) Throw in one cup of marshmallows. Be aware that the one cup line on the old measuring cup never looks like enough so always throw in an extra handful or two. My handfuls were always more accurate than Mom's because I had smaller hands!

(5) Add the milk. Open the can with a punch opener to avoid fishing the lid out of the marshmallows when you pour the milk in. (I am a can-opener-challenged person and can barely manage a manual one. Electric can openers give me nightmares). Add one-half stick of margarine and some salt to the pan. I can never remember if it is a

quarter or a half teaspoon of salt, but it is the amount that fits between two of the lines on the palm of my left hand. So, just take a good guess and go for it!

(6) Mix and stir constantly over medium heat. While doing this (remember, constant stirring is important), line a pan (whatever size you happen to have) with foil and butter it with the other half of butter stick. This should have been done at the start of the whole shebang but I always forget. I actually became quite dexterous at stirring and lining and buttering all at once. I can even stand on one foot and slam the refrigerator door shut with the other one while all this is going on!

(7) Cook mixture for five minutes. Begin timing the five minutes any time you please, but Mom and I generally started when the marshmallows began to do something in the pan. Then we usually go over by another minute or so just to be safe.

(8) When fudge looks and feels right (this gets easier to judge after a few batches), turn off burner and add vanilla, chips and nuts all at the same time. The recipe calls for one teaspoon of vanilla but you can just dump some into the wooden spoon and then dribble a little extra by mistake. Stir like crazy until it looks and smells yummy and then pour it into a pan, preferably the one you already lined with foil.

(9) Quickly scrape all remaining fudge from pan and begin layering this onto a small saucer. This fudge tastes the best and should never, ever be wasted. It is best to eat this hot while it still can burn your tongue and then wash it down with a cold glass of milk. Score the pan of fudge with a sharp knife and cut it into pieces as soon as it acts like fudge. Always eat one corner of each batch to be sure it fudged. Be prepared to have at least one batch that doesn't work (is it any wonder?) and be glad that it makes great ice cream topping.

(10) Give away fudge in tins, boxes and any other way it looks pretty to everyone you know. Remind yourself that since you only sampled corner pieces and scrapings (fewer calories than the real thing), it is okay to save a tin for yourself!

While making fudge is not the essence of what Christmas is all about, it is one small part of a tradition that taught me about joy. It was only a few hours from the fudge pan to the Christmas Eve candlelight worship service. Both were traditions that I shared with my mother, and as I grew, the fudge took on less meaning as the worship took on more.

I am thankful to my mother for establishing traditions that gave delight and joy, and that also led me to the true meaning of Christmas. I pray that I can do the same for my children. The tastes, smells, sounds, and sights of Christmas are just a hint of the glories of heaven. God became man to save us from our sins and to share with us an eternity of that glory. That is the miracle we celebrate every December. May we carry this in our hearts all year long, and if that means making fudge on the Fourth of July to remember the Christmas miracle, then so be it! "But the angel said to them, 'Do not be afraid. I bring you good news of great joy that will be for all the people. Today in the town of David a Savior has been born to you; he is Christ the Lord" (Luke 2:10-11 NIV).

A Mother's Day Letter to Mom

Spring is a time of renewal and rejuvenation. In our house it is a time of dandelion bouquets offered from grubby little hands. It is a time of hugs from little boys who smell like trees and fresh cut grass and sand and sunshine. Spring is also a time of reflection and taking stock, as it signals one more anniversary of my mother's death, one more Mother's Day without Mom at the end of the phone. This year has been especially poignant, and once again I find myself wishing I could just have a long conversation with my mom. Therefore, I am indulging myself. My Mother's Day present to myself is this column, this letter to my mom.

Dear Mom, hi there. As always, I miss you. I can't believe how fast time is going now since your death. I remember the time of your illness and the events surrounding your death as vividly as if it was yesterday. Our last hug, our last phone call, our last "I love you" still echo in my brain. I remember how many times you thanked me for staying with you and helping you, almost as if you knew you wouldn't be seeing me again. I think I knew too, because I wanted to run back and hug you one more time on that day before you died. As I headed my car back to Cheboygan, I convinced myself that it wouldn't matter, because sooner or later there would have to be a last hug, and that it would just scare you if I did turn back. I told myself that of course I would see you again, even if it was in a hospital one final time. Thirty hours later you had died and I was wishing I could turn the clock back and get that last hug.

I've grown and changed from that experience. The Lord has helped me forgive myself for not turning back, yet I do things differently now. I don't take anyone for granted. I listen to that still small voice telling me to call someone or to write a note. This new permission to be more loving and expressive, to make contact even when it seems silly, has helped a lot, especially where my father is concerned. Mom, you would be so happy at the new closeness between Dad and me. Although he hurt all of us deeply, you never said a bad word about him in my presence, and you always reminded me that no matter what happened, he was still my father. Now that I am a wife and mother, I have a little bit better understanding of the grace and dignity that took. I called Dad tonight, even though he has asked me to spare my telephone bill. He has been in the hospital most of this last month. His lungs, his heart, his diabetes are all taking a beating from the chemo. They say they're defeating the cancer, but the rest of his body is falling apart. Anyway, he faces a nasty procedure tomorrow and I just suddenly knew I wanted to hear his voice. I'm sure he'll do fine, but just in case, I wanted to tell him again that I love him. Imagine that, Mom! I can finally tell my dad that I love him, freely and without reservation. What a treat!

My big brother and I are closer also. I know that makes you happy. We always felt a loyalty that defied understanding, but it has only been since your sickness and death that we have reached out to each other. Good things really can come out of grief if we allow God to work in us. But you always knew that, didn't you? Even in your hardest times, even when you were depressed, you never lost your faith, and in the last year of your life your faith glowed. Thank you for that example Mom, and I pray that someday Russ will come to share that faith.

You would be very happy with the direction of my own life. Larry and I and the boys are thrilled to be a family, just as thrilled as we were when we first brought our little guys home from the adoption agency. Even on hard days, when I find myself burying pet iguanas and trying to convince little boys that a swig of pickle juice doesn't count as a vegetable, I rejoice in being a mom. (They must have *gotten their strange tastes from you. Remember your mashed potato sandwiches?) Well, Mom, I could go on for hours and hours, but mainly I just wanted to say Happy Mother's Day, to you from me, and to me from you. I was greatly blessed by you, because no matter how ucky things got at home, I always knew you were proud of me and that you loved me. That was a rare and special gift, and I thank you. Love, Karen.*

"As a mother comforts her child,
so will I comfort you..." (Isaiah 66:13a NIV).

A Christmas Column

    Well, I did it again. Once again Christmas has come and gone, and everything that had to be done, did get done. The presents that took hours to wrap got unwrapped in a half hour. My guys were delighted with their gifts, and we enjoyed a wonderful Christmas Day together. More importantly, we worshipped together and rejoiced as we celebrated the birth of our Savior. As a matter of fact, I felt so much Christmas joy this year that I am still bubbling over with it, just like a kid who is ready to burst. I've been more aware than ever of my many blessings, and how precious these days together really are.

    I had a moment on Christmas night when I got teary as I realized again how fast my boys are growing up, and I just wanted to tell someone all that was in my heart. When I get like this, the only thing that helps is to pen a letter to Mom. I still miss her and think about her every day, although I am doing much better now. Since I can't share things in person with her anymore, it helps to write it down. Here, then is a Christmas and a New Year's Greeting to my mom:

    Dear Mom, Merry Christmas and Happy New Year. I can't believe how fast this year has sped by. I remember when I was a kid and experienced those days of boredom that almost every kid complained about. You told me to enjoy them because I would never have those long, boring days once I was a grown up. Guess what? You were right! I may not have realized back then how smart you were, but I sure appreciate it now that I am a parent!

    Anyway, this year is almost over and so are the holidays. You would be so proud of me this year, Mom. I had a little Christmas party two days before Christmas, and I entertained just like you taught me. I made enough food to feed an army, and I got out all of those wonderful glass party dishes that belonged to you. In addition

Love, Hugs, and Kisses 127

to the ones you owned, I also have the dishes that belonged to Grandma, plus some sets that people have given me over the years. It was fun getting all of them out, and setting the table with pretty tablecloths and dishes. The party went well, with only a few minor glitches that most of the guests didn't even realize. The toilet clogged once, but since I am the queen of the plunger that was quickly resolved. You would have hated these new toilets, Mom. They just don't have enough force behind them to do the job. However, some good comes of everything, and I am now amazingly proficient with the plunger. While that topic wasn't exactly my idea of party conversation, a few of us had a good laugh about it that night. It was a good thing I got the toilet plunged when I did, because the next thing I knew my little guy was in the bathroom, being sick. He had choked on a piece of candy, but fortunately, other than a sore throat and tossing his cookies, no harm was done. He was embarrassed and weepy for a while, but cheered up before the party ended. The only other minor glitch was when somehow the bottle of blue glass cleaner under the kitchen sink sprung a leak. It spread out on the floor in front of the kitchen cabinets, but my husband noticed it before anyone stepped in it. He wiped it all up and that particular spot of linoleum is the cleanest it has ever been! Anyway, in spite of these minor little troubles, everyone had a good time, including the host and hostess! Even better, I had enough leftovers so that I didn't have to cook on Christmas Eve or Christmas Day!

    The rest of the holiday was relaxed and peaceful. I even had all of my presents wrapped before church on Christmas Eve. For the first time ever in my married history, I wasn't wrapping gifts late at night on Christmas Eve! On the way to church that night, we were all laughing hysterically at the antics of my littlest guy. Mom, sometimes I long for the calm, dignified approach that you brought to such things as bodily functions. I don't know if it is because I am surrounded by men, but sometimes I really miss the politeness that you tried so hard to instill in us. Anyway, there was nothing dignified about our conversation in the car on the way to church that night. We had pointed out a glowing Santa in a window display to our youngest, and he matte- of-factly stated, "I'm busy right now, picking my nose." We all burst into laughter as I explained for the umpteenth time that God created tissues just for that reason. My son countered with the argument that tissues don't work as well as a finger. My older son chimed in at that point about the virtues of nose picking, and it was all downhill from there. Fortunately, we did settle down by the time we arrived at church, and we enjoyed a worshipful service together. I thought of you as I watched a little girl in her Christmas finery. She held her candle so carefully as she stood by her mother, and it reminded me of you and me all those years ago. I remember feeling so proud that you trusted me to hold my candle all by myself while we sung "Silent Night." We made good memories, Mom, and I thank you for those!

  Well, it is time to end this, and to get ready to start the New Year. I have no idea what lies ahead, but I am sure it will be an adventure. I also know that I will still miss you, but that missing you is okay now. I pray that the Christmas joy of this moment will live on in all of our hearts for the next twelve months. After all, God's love is eternal, and so should be our joy!

Happy New Year, Mom.
Love, Karen.

  "My lips will shout for joy when I sing praise to you—
  I, whom you have redeemed" (Psalm 71:23 NIV).

Acknowledgments

As this book was coming to an end, I told my husband that I was having difficulty with this page. Many, many people have helped and supported me, and I just didn't know how to thank all of them. He cheerfully told me that it wasn't a problem and to just say, "Thanks everybody!" That all-enveloping thank-you does ensure that no one is excluded from my gratitude, but there remain a few that I must single out.

To my family: My husband, sons, in-laws, and aunties. "Thanks" does not begin to cover the depth of the love and gratitude I feel for all of you. You're the greatest, and at the very top of my blessing list!

To my cheering section: Those who knew me then and those who know me now: Lynn, Cathie, Laurel, Diane, Bonnie, Ellen, Marna, Jeanie, Ellie and Toni. You have prayed, cried, and laughed with me. You each have a special place in my heart, and I am grateful.

Finally, there are couples who throughout the years have loved and supported us in countless ways. Without them, this book would never have happened. To Jenny and Jeff, Jan and Mark, Marilyn and Rocky, Dan and Renee: You have allowed your faith in

Jesus Christ to shine as a beacon and encouragement in our lives. Larry and I have blossomed in large part because of your prayers, love, and encouragement. God is always faithful, and your friendship is one of the many ways in which He has lavished his grace upon us.

To anyone else not listed but who holds a place in my heart, I now quote Larry and say, "Thanks, everybody!"

Resources

<u>Local</u>

Hospice: Contact any local Hospice program. Most will have bereavement programs in place or can make a referral. Hospice programs are usually listed in the yellow pages of the phone book either under "Hospice" or "Home Health Services."

Mental Health Services: Again, listed in the yellow pages of the phone book. Most areas have a community mental health program that can provide individual counseling or make a referral.

Christian Counseling: May be listed in the phone book under "Counseling". If not, most churches will have a referral source or will directly provide counseling. If not affiliated with a local church, but desiring Christian counseling, contacting the local Christian radio station is a good place to start. Generally, they will have a listing of Christian resources available in the area.

Help can also be found by contacting your family doctor. Most doctors will determine if depression that requires treatment is present, and/or can make a referral for counseling as needed.

Michigan

> Michigan Hospice & Palliative Care Organization
> 6015 W. St. Joseph Highway, Suite 104
> Lansing, MI 48917
> email: mihospice@aol.com
> web site: www.mihospice.org

National

> Bereavement Magazine
> 8133 Telegraph Drive
> Colorado Springs, CO 80920
> (719)282-1948
>
> National Hospice Organization
> 1901 N. Moore St., Suite 901
> Arlington, VA 22209
> (703)243-5900
>
> National Association of Social Workers
> 750 1st Street N.E., Suite 7
> Washington, DC 20002
> (202)408-8600

Internet: griefnet@griefnet.org